Extraordinary from the Ordinary

Ceil Lucas, General Editor

VOLUME 1	*Sociolinguistics in Deaf Communities*
VOLUME 2	*Multicultural Aspects of Sociolinguistics in Deaf Communities*
VOLUME 3	*Deaf Children in Public Schools*
VOLUME 4	*Pinky Extension and Eye Gaze: Language Use in Deaf Communities*
VOLUME 5	*Storytelling and Conversation: Discourse in Deaf Communities*
VOLUME 6	*Bilingualism and Identity in Deaf Communities*
VOLUME 7	*Sociolinguistic Variation in American Sign Language*
VOLUME 8	*Turn-Taking, Fingerspelling, and Contact in Signed Languages*
VOLUME 9	*Language and the Law in Deaf Communities*
VOLUME 10	*To the Lexicon and Beyond: Sociolinguistics in European Deaf Communities*
VOLUME 11	*The Rising of Lotus Flowers: Self-Education by Deaf Children in Thai Boarding Schools*
VOLUME 12	*Multilingualism and Sign Languages: From the Great Plains to Australia*
VOLUME 13	*Sign Languages in Contact*
VOLUME 14	*Hearing, Mother Father Deaf: Hearing People in Deaf Families*
VOLUME 15	*Extraordinary from the Ordinary: Personal Experience Narratives in American Sign Language*

Extraordinary from the Ordinary

Personal Experience

Narratives in American

Sign Language

Kristin Jean Mulrooney

GALLAUDET UNIVERSITY PRESS

Washington, D.C.

Sociolinguistics in Deaf Communities

A Series Edited by Ceil Lucas

Gallaudet University Press
Washington, D.C. 20002

http://gupress.gallaudet.edu

© 2009 by Gallaudet University
All rights reserved.
Published in 2009
Printed in the United States of America

Cover design by Heather L. Truelove

The video clips in figures 2.12–2.14, 2.16–2.18, 3.2, 3.6b–d, 3.7–3.8a, 3.9b, 3.10b, 3.11, 3.13, 4.1–4.13, 5.1, 5.2, 5.4, 5.7, 5.11, 5.13a, 5.14a–b, 5.16, 6.2, 6.6b, 6.9, 6.10, 6.14, 6.15, 6.18, 6.21, 6.24, 6.28, 6.30, 7.3, 7.4, 8.4, and 8.6 are from the NSF-funded project on Sociolinguistic Variation in ASL (SBR-9310116 and SBR-9709522). Used with permission of Ceil Lucas, project director. All other clips are from the author's research.

ISBN 978-1-56368-416-6; 1-56368-416-0
ISSN 1080-5494

∞ The paper used in this publication meets the minimum requirements of American National Standard for Information Sciences–Permanence of Paper for Printed Library Materials, ANSI Z39.48-1984.

Contents

Editorial Advisory Board, vii

Acknowledgments, ix

CHAPTER 1 Narrative Analysis, 1

CHAPTER 2 Theoretical Background, 22

CHAPTER 3 Analyzing Narratives, 40

CHAPTER 4 A Prototypical Narrative, 53

CHAPTER 5 The Structure of Introduction and Background Sections in ASL Narratives, 70

CHAPTER 6 The Structure of Main-Event Sections in ASL Narratives, 95

CHAPTER 7 The Structure of Explication, Reflection, and Conclusion Sections in ASL Narratives, 129

CHAPTER 8 Conclusion, 145

References, 161

Appendix, 169

Index, 171

Editorial Advisory Board

Robert Bayley
Department of Linguistics
University of California, Davis
Davis, California

Jeffrey E. Davis
College of Education, Deaf
  Studies and Educational
  Interpreting
University of Tennessee
Knoxville, Tennessee

Trevor Johnston
Department of Linguistics
Macquarie University
Sydney, Australia

Susan M. Mather
Department of Linguistics
Gallaudet University
Washington, D.C.

Carolyn McCaskill
Department of ASL and Deaf
  Studies
Gallaudet University
Washington, D.C.

Stephen M. Nover
Center for ASL/English Bilingual
  Education and Research
Gallaudet University
Washington, D.C.

Lourdes Pietrosemoli
University of the Andes
Merida, Venezuela

Claire L. Ramsey
Teacher Education Program
University of California, San Diego
La Jolla, California

John Rickford
Department of Linguistics
Stanford University
Stanford, California

Adam Schembri
Deafness, Cognition and Language
  Research Centre
University College London
London, United Kingdom

Laurene Simms
Department of Education
Gallaudet University
Washington, D.C.

Graham H. Turner
Translation and Interpreting
  Studies
Heriot-Watt University
Edinburgh, Scotland

Elizabeth Winston
Educational Linguistics Research
  Center
Loveland, Colorado

Acknowledgments

I cannot compose a sentence that will adequately express the gratitude I feel toward the individuals who contributed to the completion of this book. I will make an attempt and hope you can feel my appreciation.

Thank you to the six narrators that produced these delightful tales that I had the privilege of analyzing. Your stories provided me the opportunity to learn. It will be impossible for me to ever repay you for this gift. I can only offer you my thanks.

I am also indebted to my dissertation chair, Scott Liddell, who guided me through this journey with great patience. His investment in my development as a scholar has been tremendous. I hope that in my role as a professor I will be able to inspire and challenge students as he has done for me.

The members of my committee, Robert E. Johnson, Sarah Taub, and Arlene Blumenthal Kelly, thank you for your comments and insights. To Ceil Lucas, this series editor, and Ivey Wallace, my editor, your feedback has improved this work tremendously.

I was fortunate to be taught by the talented faculty in both the Gallaudet University and the Georgetown University linguistics departments. Thank you to the professors in both these departments. In particular, I would like to thank Heidi Hamilton who sparked my interested in personal narratives and provided me the tools to analyze them.

My fellow classmates at Gallaudet University and Georgetown University, your support over the years sustained me. I am grateful to have been fortunate enough to make the journey with you.

To my parents, you instilled in me a passion for learning. I hope you know that this achievement is as much yours as mine. And my siblings, you each inspire me; I have been blessed with such a large cheering section.

Finally, to my three miracles: Aida and James, you are my precious angels. It is an honor being your mother. Jamie, you have made all this possible. Thank you, my love.

Chapter 1

Narrative Analysis

Personal narratives are one way people code their experiences and convey these experiences to others. Given that narratives simultaneously express information and define a social situation, analyzing how and why people structure the telling of personal narratives provides insight into the social dimensions of language use.

Stokoe (1960) clearly demonstrated that American Sign Language (ASL) is a natural language. *A Dictionary of American Sign Language on Linguistic Principles* (Stokoe, Casterline, and Croneberg, 1965) further documented this language. Since this groundbreaking work was published, linguists studying ASL and other signed languages have demonstrated that sign languages express the same kinds of information or ideas spoken languages convey. It should be possible, then, to analyze ASL narratives and identify how ASL users structure their stories to similarly express social dimensions. That is the focus of this volume.

STRUCTURALIST NARRATOLOGY

The backdrop to discourse analysts' work on narrative begins with Vladimir Propp's examination of Russian fairytales. *Morphology of the Folktale*, published in Russian in 1928 but not translated into English until 1958, describes the structure of these tales. Propp found that although folktales are about different incidents, they all have a similar underlying theme. He identified 31 different plot elements that consistently occur in these tales. These plot elements have been simplified by scholars (e.g., Gilet, 1998) to the following six fundamental meaningful actions:

1. Protagonist has initial harmony.
2. Protagonist discovers a lack.
3. Protagonist goes on a quest.
4. Protagonist finds helpers/opponents.
5. Protagonist is given tests.
6. Protagonist is rewarded or a new lack develops.

Propp's technique for demonstrating what all fairytales have in common and how they differ constitutes a linguistic analysis of narratives. He points out that although tales differ in detail, the themes they convey are similar. One tale may describe what happens to a prince and another the adventures of a frog. The prince may search for a mate and the frog a lily pad, but both are on a quest. Propp shows that although characters and details vary from one fairytale to the next, the more abstract plot components are similarly structured.

The work of Claude Lévi-Strauss (1955, 1964, 1966) also contributed to the understanding of narrative structure. Lévi-Strauss was interested in describing the abstract elements of meaning expressed in myths. He argued that while myths told in different languages vary widely, all deal with a limited number of basic themes that are based on binary pairs: male and female, life and death, raw and cooked. He argued that the existence of these opposites provides the basis of the structure of myths. Barthes (1966) later applied the work of Propp and Lévi-Strauss to the analysis of literary narrative.

Labov and Waletzky (1967) furthered the goal of describing underlying structures in narrative, but they differed from Propp and Lévi-Strauss in two significant ways. First, they analyzed personal experience narratives rather than fairytales. Second, they focused on the functions of individual clauses rather than larger chunks of text. They argued that folktales codified themes and structures that exist in the narratives people tell each other in daily interactions. To understand how humans organize their thought, they undertook an analysis of the source of these themes. Labov and Waletzky's work has been the most influential in American studies of narrative structure because it demonstrates how personal narratives have consistent and analyzable structure. Labov and Waletzky shifted analysts' focus from literary text to narratives produced in everyday speech.

PERSONAL NARRATIVES

Labov and Waletzky first identified personal narratives as a type of discourse while conducting research on African American Vernacular English in South Harlem. They found that one of the most successful ways to elicit examples of vernacular speech was to ask subjects to tell stories about their personal experiences.

Labov and Waletzky define personal narrative as "one method of recapitulating past experience by matching a verbal sequence of clauses to the sequence of events which actually occurred" (20). They claim that the narrative is the prototype of a well-formed speech event with a beginning, middle, and end and is composed of two types of clauses. *Referential* or *narrative* clauses describe what the story is about: events, characters, and settings. *Evaluative* or *free* clauses have to do with why the narrator is telling the story and why the audience should listen to it. The ways people structure these two types of clauses determines the overall narrative structure. Narrative clauses cannot be moved without changing the order in which events must be taken to have occurred; the two clauses "I pushed the girl and she pushed me" describe a different sequence of events than "The girl pushed me and I pushed her." Free clauses serve other functions such as evaluation.

According to Labov and Waletzky, a complex narrative includes clauses or sets of clauses that serve the following functions and typically occur in this order: abstract, orientation, complicating action, evaluation, resolution, and coda. The *abstract* summarizes the story to come. The *orientation* introduces characters, the temporal and physical setting, and the situation. The *complicating action*, the main body of narrative clauses, relays the sequence of events leading up to the climax. The *evaluation* clauses state what is interesting or unusual about the story; they justify why the person is telling the story. The *resolution* tells what happened next. Finally, the *coda* provides a short summary of what happened and connects the story to the setting in which it is being told.

Labov (1972) considers evaluation clauses to be free clauses because they can occur throughout the narrative without changing the sequence of events within the narrative. They can be interspersed throughout the narrative and provide different types of information. They may make a comment about the story such as "It was just the weirdest sight." They may also provide extra details about characters. Evaluative clauses may suspend the action and repeat or paraphrase what has happened.

Labov's analysis of narratives that were produced in real time was groundbreaking. Whereas traditional work on narratives had focused on the structure of narratives found in literary works (Lévi-Strauss 1955, Propp 1968), Labov and Waletzky showed how stories told informally were structured and could be described. The focus of linguistic research during the late 1950s and into the 1960s was on the generative revolution introduced by Chomsky (1957, 1965) that focused on finding structure up to the level of the sentence. Generative linguists were not generally interested in how language was structured in connected talk. Labov and Waletzky's observations about personal narrative structure opened up the possibility of analyzing other types of discourse.

Another of Labov and Waletzky's significant contributions was the demonstration that personal experience narratives are not told merely to convey referential information; they also function to create rapport with the audience. The fact that evaluative clauses are present in narratives supports the idea that narrator uses the narrative to connect the event with his audience in some way.

This work on narratives initiated discussion of the structure of narratives told in daily interactions. Later, the work of van Dijk and Kintsch, for example, attempted to create a model for how people produce and comprehend stories (van Dijk 1977, 1980; Kintsch and van Dijk 1975). Van Dijk defines a narrative as a type of action discourse with a point. He uses the term *macro-structures* to refer to the notion of themes or plots in literary discourse or to Labov and Waletzky's division of the narrative into the abstract or the complicating action. The difference, van Dijk explains, is that the determination of macro-structures derives from the analysis of action in the discourse. He observes 19 rules that people follow in the telling of a narrative. The rules include the following:

1. Names are generalized and substituted by indefinite descriptions or variables, e.g., "a man," "somewhere in Italy," "in an Italian village."
2. Location descriptions are deleted or integrated, e.g., "in a (beautiful) village."
3. Full identifying propositions are reduced to arguments (i.e., noun phrases in summary sentences), e.g., "there lived a rich man," "a rich man."
4. Summarizing propositions in the text are deleted, as is all redundant information.
5. All preparatory actions that are not presupposed by other propositions of the story are deleted. (van Dijk 1976, 564)

Van Dijk agrees with Labov and Waletzky that the general structure of narratives includes an orientation, complicating action, and resolution. He goes beyond this analysis to propose explicit rules to determine what information is conveyed in these categories.

Dell Hymes (1981) analyzed Native American oral narratives and discovered that they are organized in terms of lines, groups of lines, verses, and stanzas, rather than paragraphs. His work, along with others such as Chafe (1985), introduced the practice of producing transcripts that reflect how a story is told. The creation of transcripts that reflect the real-time production of a narrative has been widely adopted in narrative research. Transcripts capture the disfluencies that often occur when telling a story, but they also offer tremendous insight into their production. Hymes and Chafe demonstrate how the production of a transcript can influence the analysis. If a transcript omits false starts or other disfluencies, the analysis will omit them as well.

PHENOMENA OF NARRATIVES: EVENTS VS. NARRATIVE EVENTS

Narratives are never objective retellings of an event (Chafe 1994; Tannen 1989). The retelling is a recreation of the event in which some details of what happened are omitted while others are not. Some details may have been more salient for the narrator during the event than others. Imagine two people discussing a meeting they had both attended. One participant's narrative about what transpired at the meeting may include details about how people were dressed. The second participant may never mention people's attire but rather focus on how they were seated in the room. These differences may be attributed to what each person noticed or deemed significant. It is also possible that the differences in the two narratives reflect what the participants remember; this is another reason why narrative events may differ from the actual event. The length of time between the event and the retelling may further impact what can be remembered, as well as the accuracy of the recollection. Another influence on what narrative events are included is the point that the narrator is trying to make. In the example of the people who attended a meeting, one participant's narrative may have included a comment on how one person's outfit was unusual in some way. The other participant, however, may have been concerned with making the point that she felt slighted by where she had to sit.

The addressee of the narrative also has an influence (Bell 1984). A story told to a group of friends at the dinner table is often different than a story about the same event told to a coworker. The addressee has different background knowledge that impacts what the narrator must include in his or her story. The group of friends may be familiar with the narrator's family; the narrator can use a sibling's name and the friends will know the sibling's occupation. A coworker would be less likely to know the names of the narrator's siblings, much less how the sibling earns a living. This information may be significant to comprehension of the narrative. The narrator must therefore explicitly mention the relevant details in the narrative told to the coworker. It is easy to see, then, that the audience can influence the telling of a narrative.

The point here is that narratives cannot be described as merely a list of ordered sequences of events as they happened. The telling is not equivalent to pushing "Play" on a videotape recorder and viewing what transpired. Not all the events that occurred will be represented. Further, the narrator may add additional information that was not part of the original events. Narratives attempt to describe events for the addressee, but these descriptions are the creation of the narrator.

Various researchers have discussed how this phenomenon of recreating an event manifests itself in narratives. One common practice is the use of what Deborah Tannen calls "constructed dialogue." In her book *Talking Voices: Repetition, Dialogue, and Imagery in Conversational Discourse* (1989) Tannen argues that dialogue presented as direct quotations is understood to be primarily the creation of the speaker, not the actual words of those to whom they are attributed. In fact, a narrator may provide dialogue for another character's thoughts, which would be impossible for the narrator to know. For example, a narrator tells a friend what happened at a basketball game. The game was won in the final seconds when a player made two free throws. The narrator may say, "So she is standing at the line. She says to herself, 'Just relax, you can make these.'" The narrator creates dialogue and attributes it to the player without knowing what the player was actually thinking at the moment she was preparing to take her free throw. Tannen uses examples like this one as evidence that narratives are reflections of one person's interpretation of what transpired.

THE HISTORICAL PRESENT IN NARRATIVES

Labov and Waletzky demonstrated that narratives can be divided into parts and that these parts serve different functions. Following Labov and Waletzky, other researchers began to examine the linguistic structures that commonly appear in narratives, for example, the historical present. When telling stories about past events, people often use both past and present tense, as in, "I *walked* home from work the other day alone. All of a sudden, this man *comes* up to me and *says* . . ." The italicized words highlight the use of both past and present tense in describing this past event. The use of the present tense to describe past events is described as the "historical present." Joos (1964), Palmer (1965), and Leech (1971) suggest that the historical present is a stylistic device used to report past events that are vivid and exciting. They argue that the historical present intensifies the story by making the audience feel as if it had been present at the time of the actual experience. They also assert that for the narrator, telling the story can feel as though he or she is reliving the experience.

Schiffrin (1981) demonstrated links between the use of the historical present and evaluative high points in a narrative. She analyzed 73 narratives and found that of the 1,288 narrative clauses within the narratives, 30 percent of the verbs were in the historical present. Using Labov and Waletzky's narrative structure to identify sections within the narratives (abstract, orientation, complicating action, evaluation, resolution, and coda), she examined where in the narratives the historical present occurred. Schiffrin did not find the historical present in external evaluation clauses, abstracts, or codas. In orientation clauses, 3 percent of the verbs were in the historical present. In the complicating action clauses, however, 30 percent of the verbs were in the historical present. Further, she found that the historical present was used 63 percent of the time when a direct quote was used, compared to 5 percent of the time when an indirect quote was used. The excerpt from a narrative reproduced in figure 1.1 provides an example of this. The narrator, Craig, uses an indirect quote in line 77 and uses the past-tense verb *said* before providing the constructed dialogue. Craig uses direct quotes in lines 79–91. He precedes each example of constructed dialogue with a verb in the historical present. These verbs appear in bold.

The verbs used in the constructed dialogue itself are not counted as examples of the historical present; they are part of the original dialogue. This excerpt illustrates Schiffrin's finding that the historical present is more often used with direct quotes than indirect quotes.

In her quantitative study, Schiffrin demonstrates how a grammatical feature of English patterns within the overall structure of the narrative. In this case she argues that the narrator uses the historical present to bring the past events into the immediate moment. In so doing, the audience can hear for itself the speaker's construction of what happened and can interpret for itself the significance of those events for the experience.

77	Craig:	And he **said** I owed him.
78	Ben:	[Laughing.]
79	Craig:	And I **say**, "Look,
80		go away,
81		you're bothering me,"
82		and he **says**, "I'm in America,
83		and America is a free country,
84		because Americans are allowed to do whatever they want."
85		And I **say**,
86		"I'm not an American.
87		You can't do whatever you want to me."
88		And he **says**,
89		"You're not an American? Where you from?"
90		And I **say**,
91		"I'm not telling you, go away."

FIGURE 1.1. *Example of constructed dialogue in which historical present is used.*

Johnstone (1987) also explored the use of historical present tense in spoken narratives. She focused her research on the alternation between *say* and *said* in the introduction of constructed dialogue. Johnstone analyzed 13 personal-experience narratives recorded during conversations. These narratives all include clear examples of verbal interactions between the narrator and figures of authority, which are recreated using constructed dialogue. The authority figures are varied and include police officers, parents, military superiors, emergency room nurses, and people older than the speaker. Johnstone's quantitative analysis of the data revealed that in about half of the interchanges narrators introduced the authority figure's dialogue with a different verb tense from the one used to introduce the non-authority figure. Johnstone defines "introducers" as clauses using the verb *say* or *go*, such as "she said" or "he goes." The exchange in figure 1.2 illustrates the use of introducers, which are in bold.

Driver:	And then **I said**, "What's the problem here?"
Police officer:	**He says**, "Well ma'am...ah...you didn't stop for that stop sign back there."
Driver:	**I said**, "What?"

FIGURE 1.2 *Examples of past and present tense introducers.*

In these exchanges, the narrators always introduce non-authority figures with the past tense of the verb *say*. They introduce authority figures either with the historical present tense or without an introducer. Johnstone suggests that the use of an introducer such as "she says" or "she goes" conveys a less formal tone than "she said." The narrator uses the informal tone when providing constructed dialogue for the authority figure reinforces his or her power over the non-authority figure. The driver in the excerpt would be considered the non-authority figure and the police officer the authority figure. The narrator introduces the driver's constructed dialogue with the past tense verb *said* and the police officer's with the present tense verb *says*. Figure 1.3 presents an example of a narrative with no introducer.

The second line, "Hey, where did you go?" is constructed dialogue for the character searching for someone. There is no introducer such as "she says" or "she said" before the constructed dialogue begins. The change in tone of the narrator's voice indicates to the addressee that this is constructed dialogue. The use of the exclamation "hey" only occurs in real or constructed dialogue, so this would also clearly identify the utterance as constructed dialogue. Johnstone's assertion is that in stories that involve interactions with figures of authority, narrators use present and past tense in dialogue introducers to mark status differences. In so doing, a narrator incorporates additional social information into the narrative.

Schiffrin (1981) and Johnstone (1987) demonstrate how a specific grammatical feature, the historical present tense, patterns within narratives. Schiffrin demonstrates that the use of historical present appears most often during the complicating action. She suggests that the frequent use of historical present during this part of a narrative creates the sense that the addressee is witnessing the action. This allows the addressee to evaluate the events for him- or herself and interpret them. Johnstone describes how the use of historical present with introducers patterns in narratives involving authority figures. She suggests that an introducer in the past tense is more formal than in the present. The narrator connects this more formal tone to the non-authority figure. In so doing, the narrator enhances

---

Narrator:	So she looks around . . .
	Hey, where did you go? [voiced with a raised pitch]
Addressee:	[Laughs.]

FIGURE 1.3 *Example of constructed dialogue without an introducer.*

the discrepancy of power between the narrator and authority figure. The grammatical structures used to tell the narrative provide insight into how the narrator conceives of the event or his or her role in it.

Telling stories is a means of recounting personal experience to others. In doing so narrators convey two types of information. First, the narrator describes what happened, or the core events. As Labov and Waletzky demonstrate, core events are presented in a consistent way. Second, narratives convey the significance of what happened. Is the narrator telling the story to justify a certain behavior? Perhaps the goal is to evoke a certain response. The use of specific grammatical devices such as the historical present, or the variation of verb tenses, are different ways that narrators can choose to convey this second type of information.

NARRATIVE ANALYSIS OF ASL

The literature on spoken-language narratives described above involves unrehearsed narratives produced in conversations or sociolinguistic interviews, in which the narrator tells a story from his or her personal experience. The literature on narratives in ASL, however, does not cover the same type of "source material." Three types of ASL narratives have been analyzed: commercially produced literary narratives, elicited narratives, and personal-experience narratives. *Commercially produced literary narratives* are folktales that have been recorded and are commercially available, for example, *Bird of a Different Feather* (Bahan and Suppalla, 1994). *Elicited narratives* are those produced when a person is asked to read a story and retell it in ASL, or when a person is shown a cartoon and asked to describe what the events the cartoon depict. These narrators are animating a story created by someone else. *Personal-experience narratives*, however, are stories told about the person's own experience. The narrator is both author and animator of the tale. Despite these differences, each narrative type can offer insight into the structure of ASL narratives.

Identifying a Line

The challenges to identifying a line in a narrative have been discussed in the literature on spoken narrative (Hymes 1981, Chafe 1980). The same challenges exist when analyzing ASL narratives. When a narrative is being signed, is it possible to identify smaller parts from the stream of signs that are produced? The underlying assumption of a narrative analysis is that the narrative is not an indivisible sequence of signs, so the early work on ASL narratives focused on finding a means of identifying the beginning and end of a line.

Researchers were interested in describing how users of a gestural language structure narratives. Gee and Kegl (1983) applied a system for identifying the smallest units comprising the narrative, the line. The narrative was produced by a deaf native signer of ASL to a fluent deaf user of ASL and was one of several spontaneous narratives collected. Gee and Kegl made a transcript using English glosses, which included the duration of pauses between signs measured by the number of video fields that elapsed from the end of one sign to the beginning of the next. They then identified the longest pause, at which point they bisected the text. The same process was then applied to each unit yielded by the previous bisection. They continued this process until there were no more large pauses (defined as greater than 51 video fields or .94 seconds).

Gee and Kegl derived a hierarchical tree structure from the bisected texts (figure 1.4). Each terminal node in this tree represents a sentence. Each higher node corresponds to the narrative function of the lower-level sentences. The highest node represents the full text. The first division under this parent node identifies the *introduction* and *main story*. This continues down to the individual sentences. The meaning of each line is represented in English at the terminal node. Gee and Kegl conclude is that the pause structure in ASL narratives corresponds to the narrative structure such that longer pauses occur between the largest units of the narrative and pauses become progressively smaller as the discourse units they occur between become smaller.

Bahan and Supalla (1995) analyzed the narrative *Bird of a Different Feather* with the goal of determining if there was any pattern in the distribution and regularity of eye-gaze behavior related to line segmentation. They also addressed the issue of whether or not other behaviors, such as pausing, also could be used to identify the end of a line. Finally, they examined the interaction between eye-gaze behaviors and other nonmanual aspects of signing. For instance, did a pause always accompany a change in eye gaze at the end of a line? The 30-minute video of the narrative was divided into smaller narrative units following a system developed by Gee (1986, 1991) for spoken-language oral narratives. In this system narratives are broken down into hierarchical units in ascending order: *lines, stanzas, strophes,* and *sections*. Bahan and Supalla added two additional units to

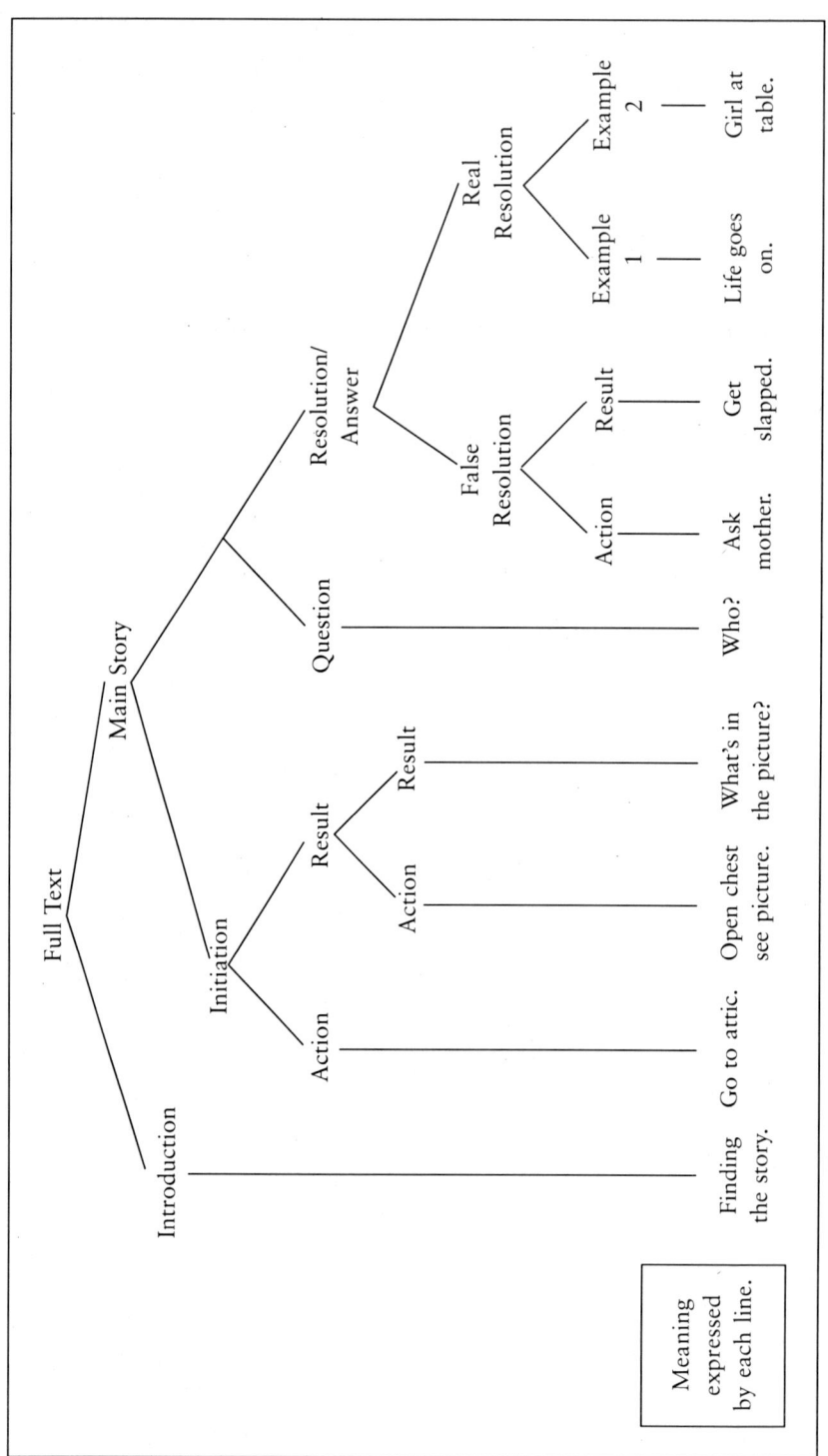

FIGURE 1.4 *Gee and Kegl's hierarchical tree structure (1983).*

their analysis, *chapters* and *parts,* because the narrative they analyzed was longer than the spoken narratives used to develop the system.

The transcript Bahan and Supalla produced included eye gaze and other nonmanual behaviors. Three types of eye-gaze behavior were recorded: gaze to the audience, gaze in the role of a character, and gaze at hands. They recorded nonmanual behaviors such as head nods and eye blinks. They also documented the lengths of pauses. They selected fifty-seven lines from the full transcript for analysis (strophes 83–90) and described patterns found for eye-gaze behavior. First, they found that if a line ends with a gaze to the audience, then the next line will begin with eye gaze at the hands or eye gaze in the role of a character. Second, if a line ends with the eye gaze at the hands or in the role of a character, then the next line begins with the eye gaze to the audience. They note that while this pattern occurred frequently in their data, line breaks were not always marked with an eye-gaze change. If eye-gaze change did not occur then other nonmanual behaviors such as pauses, head nods, and eye blinks marked line breaks.

The work of Gee and Kegl and Bahan and Supalla demonstrates that it is possible to identify lines within an ASL narrative. ASL narratives are not continuous streams of signs, but are composed of smaller units that are identifiable as lines.

Dividing a Narrative into Sections

In order to develop a preliminary description of the structure of an ASL narrative and to identify characteristics of different elements of the narrative, Wilson (1996) examined a single personal-experience narrative. The narrative is about a student who ignores school rules and chews tobacco during class. Wilson applied two approaches used in the analysis of spoken language narratives to her ASL data. She used Labov's system to divide the narrative into its component parts based on function, and she used Gee and Kegl's pause-duration technique to divide the narrative into hierarchical units.

Wilson created a glossed transcription of the story that also included nonmanual features such as facial expressions and length of pauses. A pause was considered to be an interval of time in which the handshape of the previous sign is no longer held, but the handshape of the next sign has not begun to form, or an interval during which a facial expression is held without a subsequent sign being articulated.

Using Labov's approach she divided the narrative into orientation, complicating action, and evaluation sections. She then reexamined the narrative applying Gee and Kegl's system of dividing the story based on pause length. This allowed her to divide the narrative into two halves. The first half was the description of the student's misbehavior and the second half conveyed how the student was caught. She turned to other means to divide the narrative into strophes and stanzas. These included identifying constructed dialogue, discourse markers, and referent and theme changes as boundary markers. Wilson concludes that this work demonstrates that the ASL narrative is not a unitary whole, but rather has an internal structure that includes subsections of certain lengths. She notes that the narrator in this case used constructed dialogue frequently, and points to constructed dialogue as an essential means of identifying the structure of ASL narratives.

Constructed Dialogue and Constructed Action

Metzger (1995) examined the occurrence of constructed dialogue and constructed action in ASL narratives. In her study she uses Tannen's (1989) 10 types of constructed dialogue to see if ASL makes use of the same categories. These categories are listed in figure 1.5.

Tannen defines constructed action as depictions of both physical and mental events. For instance, a narrator telling a story about a letter he wrote may demonstrate this by moving his hand as if writing on a piece of paper. Metzger analyzed both personal experience narratives and narratives elicited from informants describing comic strips. She transcribed

1. Representing what was not said.
2. Dialogue as instantiation.
3. Summarizing dialogue.
4. Choral dialogue.
5. Dialogue as inner speech.
6. Dialogue as inner speech of others.
7. Dialogue constructed by a listener.
8. Direct/indirect quotes.
9. Vague referents.
10. Dialogue of nonhuman speaker.

FIGURE 1.5 *Categories of constructed dialogue from Tannen (1989).*

the data using English glosses and conventions for transcription of nonmanual signals that included body posture, eye gaze, head placement, and mouth, cheek, and eyebrow movement. Metzger proposes that ASL use of constructed action parallels eight of the 10 categories of constructed dialogue in figure 1.5. The two exceptions are constructed action as inner action and constructed action as inner actions of others

Metzger found examples of six of the 10 categories of constructed dialogue in the narratives she examined. She also found examples of seven of the eight constructed action categories in the same narratives. Table 1.1 summarizes the types of constructed dialogue and constructed action that she found in the ASL narratives she examined. An X indicates that an example of this category was found in the data. A ? marks the two categories that Metzger states are not possible in ASL, action as inner action and inner action of others.

Metzger then examined two narratives and compared the number of instances of constructed action and constructed dialogue. She found 25 instances of constructed action and 15 instances of constructed dialogue, which she suggests is evidence that constructed action is more common in ASL than constructed dialogue. She also notes that constructed action and constructed dialogue may co-occur. Her analysis demonstrates that constructed action is a grammatical device that is used often in ASL narratives and that constructed dialogue may be a form of constructed action.

Rayman (1999) provides additional evidence that grammatical features help shape discourse structure. She elicited stories from five native users of ASL and five native users of English. Participants viewed a two-minute silent cartoon based on Aesop's fable *The Tortoise and the Hare*. Each participant was then asked to retell the story to the researcher in their native language. Rayman selected two of the 10 narratives to examine, one using ASL and the other English. Trained actresses produced the two narratives she selected. Rayman states the following reason for comparing these two narratives:

> Looking at examples of stories that exploit linguistic resources to the fullest, we can truly examine the differences in storytelling in the visual mode and how these impact the form and content of the stories. (Rayman 1999, 66)

Her comparison of the English and ASL narratives reveals some interesting differences. The first difference she identified was that the English speaker told the majority of her story in the narrator mode while the ASL

TABLE 1.1. Instances of Constructed Dialogue or Constructed Action in ASL Narratives.

Categories of Constructed Dialogue	ASL Example of Dialogue	ASL Example of Action	Categories of Constructed Action
representing what was not said		X	representing what was not done
dialogue as instantiation		X	action as instantiation
summarizing dialogue	X	X	summarizing action
choral dialogue	X	X	choral action
dialogue as inner speech	X	?	action as inner action
dialogue as inner speech of others	X	?	inner action of others
dialogue constructed by a listener			action constructed by a listener
direct/indirect quotes	X	X	direct/indirect action
vague referents		X	vague referents
dialogue of nonhuman speaker	X	X	action of nonhuman speaker

signer told the majority of her story in character mode. Rayman does not provide a definition of narrator mode or character mode. She also does not describe how she determined when one or the other mode was being used. However, I interpret narrator mode to mean that the narrator is not using real-space blends to depict the events of the story. When Rayman refers to character mode, the narrator does use real-space blends. (Chapter 2 defines real-space blends and how they are used in ASL narratives.)

The two narratives also differed in the description of action. The ASL signer provided more elaborate description of actions than the English speaker; she often inserted depictions of actions that were not in the cartoon itself. Additionally, the ASL signer indicated the manner of movement and the spatial relationship of the tortoise and the hare through the use of role shifting and depicting verbs.[1] The English story left this underdeveloped or relied on words such as *behind*, *after*, and *in front of* to describe these details. Rayman concludes that the grammatical devices available in ASL allow ASL signers to more easily represent concepts involving physical motion or movement in space.

Gestures and Real-Space Blends

In Liddell and Metzger's (1998) study of elicited narrative, a native ASL user produced a 22-second narrative based on a cartoon. Liddell and Metzger divided the narrative into nine episodes based on the spatial conceptualizations used by the signer. Each episode corresponded to a line in the transcript.

Liddell and Metzger argue that the narrator relied not only on grammatically structured arrangements of signs, but also on spatial conceptualizations involving both the signer and the space surrounding the signer, as well as gestures making use of these conceptualizations. They describe how the narrator uses constructed action to represent characters' behavior through visual demonstration of their actions. In the eighth episode of the narrative, for example, the signer does not produce any ASL signs. Instead he flails his arms to demonstrate what the character in the story did. The interpretation of the story relied on gestures produced by the head and eyes, hands and body, and facial expressions in addition to lexical signs.

1. Rayman uses the term *classifier* in her work. She does not provide a transcript of the narratives, but it is likely she is referring to what Liddell (2003) calls *depicting verbs*.

This examination points to the need for analysis of ASL narratives to include conceptualizations of the signer and the space surrounding the signer, as well as gestures.[2]

The analyses of ASL narratives reviewed above address different aspects of the structure of ASL. Some describe how to identify individual lines. They show that eye gaze and pausing mark breaks in signing that can help identify lines. The narrative may also be divided into sections based on the type of information being conveyed. The research has also described the use of different grammatical devices such as constructed dialogue and constructed action in the narratives. Finally, it is now clear that an analysis of narratives must also include gestures and spatial conceptualizations.

WHAT CONSTITUTES DATA FOR ANALYSIS?

Imagine someone making the following command to you: "Hand me that pen." You look down and see three different pens in front of you, a red one, a blue one, and a black one. Which one do you hand to the speaker? Which pen does the phrase *that pen* refer to? It is not possible to determine which pen to give the person based solely on the words uttered. If, however, we saw the speaker point toward the blue pen while uttering the sentence, we would know which pen to hand over.

Traditionally in the field of linguistics a distinction is made between *linguistic* and *paralinguistic* information. In this view, words and how they are structured constitute linguistic data. Paralinguistic information includes variations in the intonation, stress, and articulation of words. For some analysts this term also includes any movement of the body that accompanies the uttered words.[3] Thus all four words in "Hand me that pen" fall into the category of linguistic information, whereas the gesture accompanying the statement is paralinguistic. The analysis of vocally produced narratives, with few exceptions, restricts the data for analysis to linguistic elements such as words and morphemes and omits paralinguistic information.

Because of this focus on linguistic information and the exclusion of paralinguistic information, words are given prominence. Linguists com-

---

2. A description of these conceptualizations in terms of mental space blending will be provided in chapter 2.

3. The term *kinesics* has been used to refer to "articulation of the body, or movements resulting from muscular and skeletal shifts" (Key 1975, 10). The term *co-speech gesture* is also commonly used to label gestures produced while speaking.

monly assumed that words alone are sufficient to determine the meaning and structures of a narrative. Other sources of meaning are minimized, such as how the voice is used. Does the narrator vary the volume of his or her voice? Is the pace varied? Is the pronunciation of words altered? Studies usually neglect to analyze the use of different facial expressions. Gestures that accompany any of the words are not seen as available to contribute meaning and enhance one's understanding of the narrative. The paralinguistic aspects of how a narrative is conveyed (voice quality, facial expressions, gestures, other movements of the body) are excluded if they never become part of the transcript.

McNeill (1992) and Kendon (2004) describe how gestures are used with spoken languages. McNeill's analysis includes different classifications of gestures. *Imagistic* gestures convey an image of what is being referred to. This image may be physical, such as the shape of the object or how the object moves. Other gestures are *non-imagistic*. These include deictic gestures such as pointing or rhythmic movements, which mark segments of the discourse. Gestures have different functions, and, as Kendon argues, they contribute to the meaning of the utterances in which they are part. Consider, for example, a person using the distance between his or her hands to specify size while saying, "I am looking for a piece this big." The words *this big* introduce size without being specific about actual size, while the gesture demonstrates the information about size. The contributions of both parts allow the addressee to correctly interpret the utterance.

Gestures may be excluded from most spoken narrative analysis because they do not lend themselves to easy documentation. If the example above was part of a typical sociolinguistic analysis of narrative, it would be transcribed as "I am looking for a piece this big." Documentation of the gestures might be added in parentheses, for example, "(hands held about four inches apart)." This description may not clearly describe the details of the gesture. That is, it does not specify the orientation of the hands, the extension of any fingers, etc. It also does not identify at which point in the utterance the gesture appeared. Was the gesture produced simultaneously with the utterance beginning with the word "I" or did the speaker raise his or her hands while speaking the words "this big"? The fact that analysts rely on written transcripts may limit the inclusion of gestural information in the analysis of spoken narratives.

Very detailed systems for recording the details of gestures have been developed by McNeill and his students. The transcription systems for documenting the use of gestures attempts to be as precise as possible in identifying the specific video frame in which the gesture first appears. The work of McNeill, Kendon, and others argues for the importance of gestures in language. It also provides a methodology for documenting its production.

The inconsistent appearance of paralinguistic information in sociolinguistic analyses may be due to the use of audiotape recordings to collect narrative data. Audiotape recorders preserve only what can be heard. In spite of this, the importance of including gestures in a sociolinguistic analysis has received some attention. Hinrichs and Polanyi (1986) argue that deictic gestures are necessary to the correct interpretation of discourse and therefore must be included in one's explanation of how discourse is structured.

It is a given that the signs produced in an ASL narrative must be represented in a transcript. Evidence of this is the fact that in all the studies reviewed, authors recorded a gloss for every sign articulated in the transcript. After that point there is considerable variation in what other information is documented. Body posture; eye gaze; head placement; mouth, cheek, and eyebrow movement; and facial expressions are all behaviors that contribute to the meanings of ASL narratives. These behaviors are not consistently documented in transcripts across different analyses, and it is not clear how this information impacts the analysis.

Liddell and Metzger do include descriptions of gestures used in their transcript. They also describe how signs can be directed in space. The ability to direct signs in gradient ways requires that the transcript also reflect this information. Compare, for example, the signs in figure 1.6a and b. The signer articulates two instances of the sign THERE$^{\rightarrow L}$. In figure 1.6a, the sign THERE$^{\rightarrow L1}$ is directed ahead and to the left of his body. In figure 1.6b THERE$^{\rightarrow L2}$ is directed to an area near his left shoulder. The two instances of the sign THERE$^{\rightarrow L}$ differ in their direction. A transcript that

a. THERE$^{\rightarrow L1}$ b. THERE$^{\rightarrow L2}$

FIGURE 1.6 *Example of signs being directed in space.* (See copyright page for image attribution.)

simply includes the gloss THERE will not provide the information needed for a correct interpretation of the discourse.

Sign languages are different from spoken languages in that they are perceived visually rather than aurally. The language modality requires that signing be recorded using videotape and this visual documentation must be viewed in order to conduct an analysis. A transcript in the form of English glosses traditionally does not include this visual component. The transcript may be supplemented with the information that the researcher feels is critical to the analysis or interpretation of the discourse. How this is accomplished varies somewhat, but a gloss such as THERE is typical. The gloss may be accompanied by nonmanual information such as eye gaze, furrowed brows, a shocked expression, etc.

Using English to describe what sign glosses do capture is useful but risks omission or misinterpretation of information that is important to the analysis. For instance, I have not seen details such as the following in published transcripts: THERE (hand started at neck and ended ahead of signer and at level of stomach). The description is intended to show that the sign began at a higher vertical location than it ended. This may be analogous to spoken language transcripts that do not include prosody. This detail may be treated as paralinguistic and therefore excluded from the linguistic analysis. So as not to exclude important information, it is necessary that photos and expanded glosses be included in the transcript of an ASL narrative. It is also critical to return to the video as an analysis is being conducted to minimize exclusion of paralinguistic information.

If we expand our concept of language from solely grammatical symbols to include how speakers express meaning through combinations of grammar, gestures, and other paralinguistic information, then we cannot exclude any aspect of what a speaker or signer produces. All aspects of the utterance—words (signs), gestures, tone of voice, pitch of voice, direction of a sign, facial expression—must be included in the transcript in order to not lose data important to understanding the meanings expressed in narrative.

Chapter 2

Theoretical Background

Fauconnier (1985, 1997) developed his theory of "mental spaces" to account for how we use language to construct and process meanings that go beyond what is encoded by the grammatical system. Fauconnier proposes that when we engage in any kind of discourse, we create and make use of mental spaces. These mental spaces are "constructs distinct from linguistic structures, but built up in any discourse according to guidelines provided by the linguistic expressions" (Fauconnier 1985, 16). Grammatical expressions provide cues that allow speakers and signers to create and navigate mental space structures and for the addressee to do the same.

Mental spaces are conceptualizations. I distinguish between two types of mental spaces that occur frequently in narrative data. I will refer to a recollected or imagined event as an *event space*. I will label *background knowledge* those concepts based on our understanding of the world. These two categories of mental spaces represent different types of conceptualizations and will appear frequently in the analyses that follow in later chapters.

In chapter 1 I used the sentence "Hand me that pen" to illustrate the significance of gestures in understanding the meaning partially encoded in the sentence. As he utters the sentence the speaker points toward the pen that he is requesting. When the addressee hears the sentence he or she decodes the phonetic signal and understands that the speaker would like a pen. The phonetic signal, however, does not specify who the speaker is or which pen the speaker needs. The addressee relies on the physical context to identify who the speaker is and on the pointing gesture to identify which pen to hand the speaker. Figure 2.1 illustrates how the significance of the pointing gesture is associated with the grammatical form. The circle in figure 2.1 labeled "Real Space" represents the addressee's conceptualization of the physical context in which the sentence was uttered. The pointing gesture in real space is required for full comprehension of the utterance. The words and the gesture are both produced in real space. The connection between the real-space pen and the concept encoded by *that pen* is motivated by the direction of the pointing, which is toward a pen in real space. This pointing identifies the referent associated with the

FIGURE 2.1 *How a pointing gesture pairs with grammatical form in meaning constructions.*

meaning encoded by the phrase. Figure 2.1 illustrates how concepts from mental space theory can provide a way of linking grammatically encoded meanings with the context in which an utterance is made. The result is a constructed meaning (Fauconnier 1997), which goes beyond the meanings encoded by the grammar.

BLENDED MENTAL SPACES

Mental space blending is a cognitive process that creates a new mental space from two input spaces (Fauconnier & Turner 1994, 1996; Fauconnier 1997). Blended mental spaces help in understanding more complex linguistic structures such as metaphors, metonymy, narrative structure, and speech acts. One important type of blend in the analysis of ASL is a real-space blend.

Liddell (2003, 82) describes *real space* as "a person's current conceptualization of the immediate environment based on sensory input." That is, elements of real space are conceptualized as occupying locations in the immediate environment. This is an example of a *grounded* mental space. Recollections of past events are described as *nongrounded* because the thing or events being conceptualized are not conceptualized as being in the immediate environment.

FIGURE 2.2 *Example of a sign being directed toward a person in real space.*

In ASL, specific categories of signs can be directed at elements of real space. For example, the signer on the left in figure 2.2 directs the non-first person singular pronoun PRO$^{\rightarrow a}$ toward the person on the right. This is an example of directing a pronoun toward an element of real space, or the pronoun's referent. The addressee would see where PRO$^{\rightarrow a}$ was pointing and make the connection that the pronoun refers to the man PRO$^{\rightarrow a}$ is directed toward. There is no blending in this example. The pronoun is simply directed toward an element of real space.

We map elements from a mental space onto elements of real space to create an emergent *real-space blend.* Let's imagine that my husband and I are discussing how to rearrange our living-room furniture while eating dinner. I use my spoon to represent the sofa, a saltshaker to represent a chair, and my glass to represent the living-room window. In real space the spoon, glass, and salt shaker remain a spoon, a glass, and salt shaker, but in the real-space blend they become furniture and a location in the living room. I place the glass on the table and arrange the spoon and salt shaker near it and say, "I think we should move the sofa and chair near the window like this." The arrangement of the real-space entities is illustrated in figure 2.3a. The |sofa|, |window|, |chair| and |room| are all elements of a real-space blend. The blended |living room| is a visible three-dimensional model of the proposed arrangement. The tabletop, spoon, glass, and salt shaker are in real space and blend with the concepts of the living-room floor, sofa, window, and room.

Once created, the real-space blend represented in figure 2.3b is available for use by speaker and addressee in subsequent discourse. Additional details can be added to the blend; for example, my husband could pick up a pepper grinder and place it between the spoon and glass while stating, "And the lamp should be moved here."

 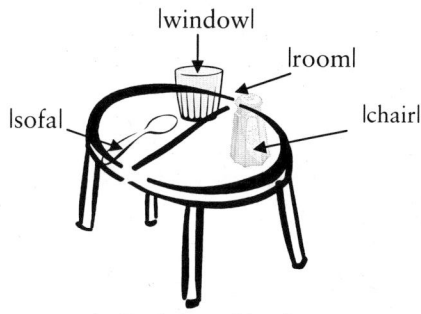

a. Real space b. Real-space blend

FIGURE 2.3 *Comparison of real space and real-space blend.*

Real-space blending is common in ASL discourse, which uses various types of real-space blends. I will focus on three commonly used blends: surrogate blends, token spaces, and depicting blends.

Surrogate Blends

A *surrogate blend* (Liddell 1995, Liddell 2003) creates entities that are imagined to be present, or surrogates. Signs can be directed at surrogates in the same manner they would be directed toward real people and things in real space. Figures 2.4 and 2.5 provide examples of two surrogate blends used in a single narrative.

The narrator is telling a story about an interaction he had at a grocery store. The store manager walks up behind him while he is shopping and gets his attention. Figure 2.4 captures the narrator's representation of the store manager getting his attention. The narrator demonstrates the manager trying to get the attention of the signer as he was shopping. His right

GET-ONE'S-ATTENTION→y
Store manager gets narrator's attention.

FIGURE 2.4 *Surrogate blend.*

Theoretical Background : 25

LOOK-AT$^{\to y}$
"He looked at the person."

FIGURE 2.5 *Surrogate blend.*

hand moves repeatedly toward an area slightly ahead of him. This verb is normally directed toward a person whose attention is requested who is physically present. In figure 2.4 there is no one in the signer's immediate environment that the verb is directed toward. This suggests he must be using a space other than real space, that is, a blended surrogate space. Within that space the signer blends with the manager and demonstrates the looking behavior of the manager. The |manager| in the blended space is trying to get the attention of the |signer shopping| in that situation at that time. The |signer shopping| is conceptualized as being in front of the |manager|. The sign is directed and produced as though someone were present. That is, the sign GET-ONE'S-ATTENTION$^{\to y}$ is directed toward the surrogate at approximately the level of the surrogate's arm or shoulder. This leads to the conclusion that the signer has conceptualized a surrogate ahead and slightly to his left.

Recall that a blend is a mental space built from separate input spaces. In a real-space blend, one of the input spaces is real space. It is grounded in the immediate environment. The other is nongrounded, that is, not part of the immediate conceptual environment. The two input spaces for the real-space blend shown in figure 2.4 are the event space and real space. The event space is the signer's conceptualization of what happened at the store. The real-space blend is presented as a partial visual demonstration of what happened. The real-space blend incorporates aspects from both these input spaces.

Figure 2.6 shows how the real-space blend is created from the two input spaces. In the surrogate blend, the narrator's face and body are blended with that of the manager in the event space. As a result, a part of the narrator becomes the visible blended entity |manager|. He also provides evidence for an invisible surrogate |signer shopping|, with his articulation of GET-ONE'S-ATTENTION$^{\to y}$ toward |signer shopping|. The narrator

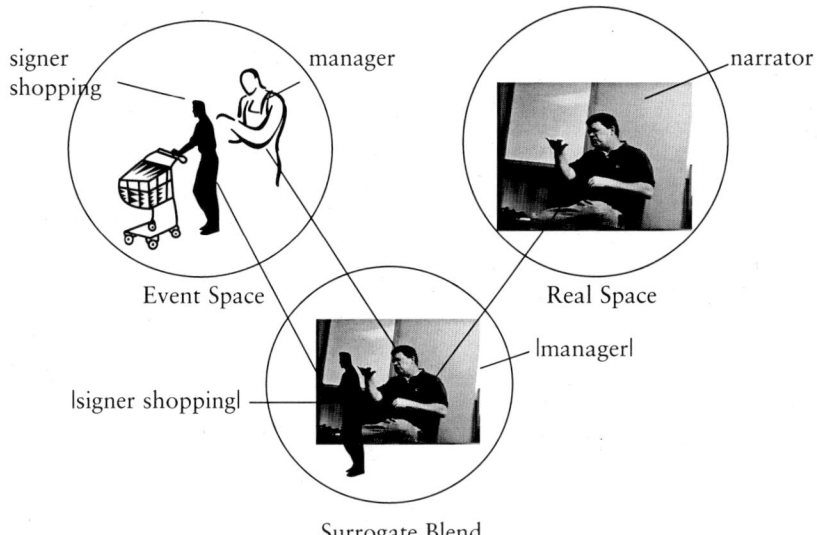

FIGURE 2.6 *Surrogate blend.*

signs GET-ONE'S-ATTENTION$^{\rightarrow y}$ at the same time his body is demonstrating through the blend what the manager did to create a real-space blend. This real-space blend includes the signer as one of the entities within the blend and thus becomes a surrogate blend. Within the blend are two surrogates, the |narrator shopping| and the |manager|.

After signing GET-ONE'S-ATTENTION$^{\rightarrow y}$ the narrator next produces LOOK-AT$^{\rightarrow y}$ (figure 2.5). The articulation of this sign signals a new surrogate blend. The event space now represents the signer's conceptualization of what happened next at the store from the perspective of the shopping narrator. This real-space blend is again a partial visual demonstration of the event, but this time from a different perspective. Figure 2.7 diagrams this new real-space blend.

Several things provide evidence that a new blend has been created. The first is the change in eye gaze. As the signer articulates LOOK-AT$^{\rightarrow y}$ he directs his eye gaze up and to his right. The narrator's expression conveys a person looking at someone else, in response to a request for attention. There is no one to the signer's right in real space with whom he could make eye contact; however, he interacts with this space in a way that reflects that he has imagined a person in this space. The narrator's facial expression has also changed. The narrator's eyebrows were furrowed and his face appeared tense when articulating GET-ONE'S-ATTENTION$^{\rightarrow y}$. While

Theoretical Background : 27

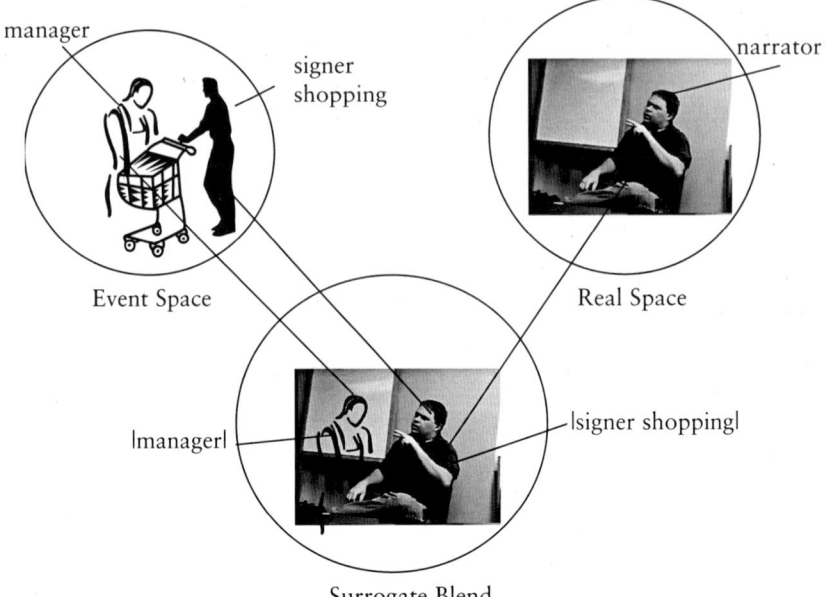

FIGURE 2.7 *Demonstration of looking at manager.*

producing LOOK-AT$^{\rightarrow y}$, however, his face and eyebrows are relaxed. The change in expression signals that the narrator is no longer demonstrating what the store manager is doing. These differences provide evidence for the existence of a new surrogate.

In figure 2.7 the narrator's body, head posture, facial expression, and eye gaze blend with his conceptualization of himself shopping. The manager in the event space blends with the space to the narrator's right. The narrator's left arm is used to sign LOOK-AT$^{\rightarrow y}$. This narration complements the demonstration in the surrogate blend. The narration explains what happened while the surrogate blend provides a partial demonstration of the same event. Since it is unlikely that the |narrator shopping| produced the sign LOOK-AT$^{\rightarrow y}$ when responding to the manager, this sign is not part of the surrogate blend.

These two examples illustrate how surrogate blends are used in ASL narratives. They also demonstrate how meaning is created from various types of signals. The meanings encoded by the signs GET-ONE'S-ATTENTION$^{\rightarrow y}$ and LOOK-AT$^{\rightarrow y}$ are important but insufficient to understanding what happened. The lexical sign, eye gaze, facial expressions, and body positions all contribute information about the event being described. Finally, the fact that they occurred in rapid sequence is evidence of how quickly and easily such conceptualizations are constructed in ASL narratives.

The examples shown in figure 2.4 and figure 2.5 also show how signers can selectively project only parts of themselves into a real-space blend. The narrator in figure 2.4 used his eye gaze, head posture, and facial expression to represent the actions of the manager while the hand and arm producing the sign were those of the narrator in real space. In figure 2.5 he uses the same projected body parts to show the narrator's response. The narrator produced the signs GET-ONE'S-ATTENTION$^{\rightarrow y}$ and LOOK-AT$^{\rightarrow y}$, both of which describe what happened and are not part of the surrogate blend. This is why the arm articulating these signs does not appear in the surrogate blend; only a partial projection of the signer appears. The ability to partition the body in blending allows for more options in the creation of real-space blends. Dudis (2004) examines which parts of the body can participate in the mappings that create blends and describes four partitionable zones: two manual articulators, the oral articulator, and facial expressions.

We have already seen examples of partitioning in figures 2.4 and 2.5. The eyes and facial expressions are partitioned to represent the actions of the manager and the narrator shopping. The right arm in figure 2.4 and left arm in figure 2.5 serve a separate function in that they describe what is happening. The addressee simultaneously sees a partial demonstration of the event and the narrator's description of the event.

Token Spaces

The narrator in figure 2.8 is telling a narrative about an experience that he had at college. The story describes a conflict between students and administrators at the university. He is describing the fact that he felt a part of a group of students by saying he and the student group were "the

a. SAME-DUAL$^{\leftrightarrow y}$

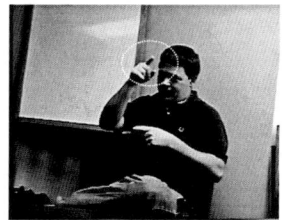
b. PRO$^{\rightarrow x}$

FIGURE 2.8 *Signs directed at a token associated with two different groups.*

same." Interestingly, he directs the sign SAME-DUAL$^{↔y}$ between himself and the space ahead of him and to his right. This supports the idea that he associates the area ahead of himself and to his right with the student group. The narrator continues by describing how he and the students defied the wishes of the administrators. He directs the sign PRO$^{→x}$ up and toward the area in front of his forehead, which demonstrates that he associates this area with the administrators. The circles in figures 2.8a and 2.8b identify the areas associated with these two groups. In figure 2.8a the sign SAME-DUAL$^{x↔y}$ moves back and forth between the narrator and an area of space associated with the student group. PRO$^{→x}$ is directed upwards in figure 2.8b and refers to administrators.

The areas represented by the circles in figure 2.8 are blends called *tokens* (Liddell 1995, 2003), which do not include the narrator. The space ahead of the narrator's right shoulder is the blended entity |students|. The space ahead and to the left of the signer's forehead is the blended entity |administrators|. Signs directed toward these tokens make reference to these entities.

Token blends differ from surrogate blends in that the signer is not part of a token blend. In addition, while surrogate blends can be very large, with surrogates located great distances from the signer, tokens are restricted to the space ahead of the signer where signs are articulated. The placement of tokens can be influenced by factors such as a power difference between different entities. In the example in figure 2.8, the administrators are associated with a location higher in the signing space than the students. This corresponds with the spatial metaphor "powerful is up," which is common in both spoken languages (Lakoff & Johnson 1980) and ASL (Taub 2001). Tokens also differ from surrogates in that they may not be interacted with as if the entities they represent are present (Liddell 2003).

Depicting Blends

Another type of blend involves depicting verbs (Liddell 2003). These verbs are articulated in space in a manner that depicts certain aspects of the verb's meaning. An example is the verb UPRIGHT-PERSON-MOVE-QUICKLY-TO$^{↓L1-L2}$ in the sequence shown in figure 2.9a, 2.9b, and 2.9c. This lexical verb means "a person quickly walks to a location." In addition to expressing this lexically fixed meaning, it also depicts the path and manner of the movement. In figure 2.9, the depicted movement starts well ahead of the signer's right shoulder and moves to his left. The signer also bends

a.   b.   c.

UPRIGHT-PERSON-MOVE-QUICKLY-TO$^{\downarrow L1\text{-}L2}$
"The student quickly walked to the building."

FIGURE 2.9 *Example of a depicting verb.*

and extends the 1 handshape during the movement. The signer moves his hand quickly to represent the rapid movement of the person walking.

Depicting verbs and depicting spaces are extremely common in ASL discourse. Signers use a sign with a specific lexical meaning and articulate it in a way that visually depicts the situation. This combination represents the narrator's conceptualization of the event in the space ahead of the signer. Liddell (2003) describes three categories of depicting verbs.

> The first consists of verbs signifying the presence of an entity at a place. Verbs in the second category signify the shape and extent of a surface or the extent of a linear arrangement of individual entities. Verbs in the third category signify movements or actions. (Liddell 2003, 262)

All three types of depicting verbs appear in the ASL narratives analyzed. Examples of each type are illustrated in figure 2.10.

In figure 2.10a the narrator begins with a description of a uniquely shaped container. The container is actually a miniature coffin, which the narrator describes with the depicting verb RECTANGULAR-CONTAINER-EXTEND-TO$^{\downarrow L1\text{-}L2}$. The sign begins with the fingertips of the two hands contacting each other to form a point. He then draws his hands back toward his body and extends his wrists causing his fingertips to point out. The sign ends with the heels of his hands near each other. The left hand remains in place when he begins the depicting verb LONG-ENTITY-BE-AT$^{\downarrow L1}$. The hand that remains in place for a semantic purpose is called a *fragment buoy* (Liddell 2003). A buoy, as described by Liddell (2003, 223), "serves as a conceptual landmark as the discourse continues." A fragment buoy is a buoy created from a fragment of the previously produced sign. In this instance, the left hand blends with the side of the coffin, thus providing a physical landmark identifying the side of the coffin. But knowing where

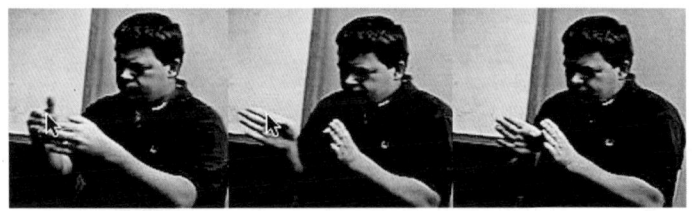
RECTANGULAR-CONTAINER-EXTEND-TO$^{\downarrow \text{L1-L2}}$

a. LONG-ENTITY-BE-AT$^{\downarrow \text{L}}$
fragment buoy (of RECTANGULAR-CONTAINER-EXTEND-TO$^{\text{L1-L2}}$)*

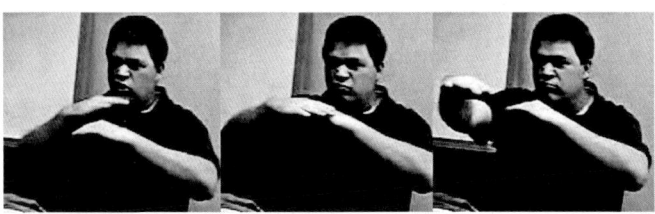

b. FLAT-BROAD-SURFACE-EXTEND-TO$^{\downarrow \text{L1-L2}}$

c. VEHICLE-DRIVE-TO$^{\downarrow \text{L1-L2}}$
   BROAD-SURFACE$^{\downarrow \text{L1}}$

*The gloss of the sign being articulated by the strong hand is placed above the gloss of the sign produced by the weak hand.

FIGURE 2.10 *Examples of the three types of depicting verbs.*

the side of the coffin is also leads to knowing where the rest of the coffin is conceptualized. The fragment buoy remains as the narrator continues. The articulation of LONG-ENTITY-BE-AT$^{\downarrow \text{L1}}$ is an example of a depicting verb that is used to express an entity at a place. The narrator uses it to describe and depict the location of a dead rat. The extended finger blends with the deceased rat. I use the notational convention developed by Liddell (2003), which allows direction and placement information to be expressed along with the English gloss. The symbol ↓L1 means that the sign is produced at the location L1.

Two hands appear in figure 2.10a. The left hand is the fragment buoy that represents the side of a container, which was described with the depicting verb RECTANGULAR-CONTAINER-EXTEND-TO↓L1-L2. The right hand now produces LONG-ENTITY-BE-AT↓L1 next to the fragment buoy. The articulation of the sign with the right hand to the right of and near the fragment buoy allows the addressee to understand that the entity was placed inside the container.

Figure 2.10b provides an example of Liddell's second category of depicting verbs. The sign FLAT-BROAD-SURFACE-EXTEND-TO↓L1-L2 describes a flat, broad surface that extends a great distance. The right hand moves to depict the extent of the surface. The shape of both hands represents the shape of the surface described. The symbol ↓L1-L2 represents the hand moving from L1 to L2. The narrator produced this sign as a part of his description of a large body of water.

The sign VEHICLE-DRIVE-TO↓L1-L2 in figure 2.10c is an example of the third category of verbs, those that show movement or action. The narrator is depicting the path his friend's bicycle took after hitting a bump in the road. The 3 handshape is part of the lexical verb expressing the movement of vehicles. Additionally it blends with the bicycle to depict the movement of the bicycle. The path of the moving hand during the production of the verb depicts the movement of the bicycle.

Partitioning can also be part of the production of depicting verbs. For example, the narrator in figure 2.11 is describing his experience competing in a biathlon. The five photos illustrate how he expressed his movement and effort while running. He signs UPRIGHT-PERSON-MOVE-QUICKLY-TO↓L1-L2, which begins near his right shoulder and moves away from his

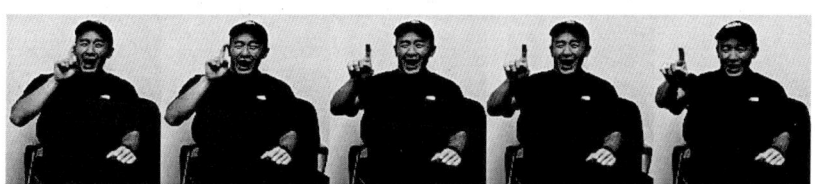

UPRIGHT-PERSON-MOVE-QUICKLY-TO↓L1-L2

FIGURE 2.11 *Partitioning in a depicting blend.*

body as he extends his arm. The verb describes a person moving quickly from one location to another. An addressee would construct the meaning *run* from the context, which is describing a biathlon in which competitors run during one part.

The narrator creates two distinct blends. His movement at the time of the biathlon is mapped onto extended upright index finger. The intense facial expression signals that a surrogate blend has been created, and it demonstrates the effort being put forth as he competes. These two real-space blends draw on the ability of signers to selectively project only parts of themselves into a real-space blend. This results in the signer conveying three types of information simultaneously. The depicting verb narrates, the depicting blend depicts, and the surrogate blend demonstrates the intensity. He depicts his own path movement through the path of the depicting verb. This creates the blended entity |runner$_1$| within the depicting blend. At the same time the narrator's facial expression conveys his intensity as he is running. This creates the surrogate entity |runner$_2$| within the surrogate blend. Thus, there are two simultaneous blended instances of himself running in the signing shown in figure 2.11.

The three types of blends that occur frequently in ASL narratives—surrogate blends, token blends, and depicting blends—appear in particular patterns in personal narratives. Their distribution will become an important part of the analysis of narrative structures in ASL.

NARRATOR MODES

The literature on both spoken and sign language makes a distinction between the narrator in the "role of narrator" versus the "role of a character"(Schiffrin 1984; Capps & Ochs 1995; Rayman 1999). Although the term has not formally been defined, *narrator role* has been aligned with utterances in a narrative that are about "what happened." In English narratives these utterances are typically in the past tense and are often evaluative clauses. In ASL they are utterances that use only lexical signs without the use of surrogate or depicting blends. The *character role* represents utterances that present what happened in a way that makes the addressee able to partially experience the event. Schiffrin (1981) has argued that this is accomplished in English by the use of the historical present and constructed dialogue. I interpret the character role to be present in ASL when surrogates or depicting verbs are used to allow a partial demonstration

| DURING | WINTER | COLD |

FIGURE 2.12 *Signer in the narrator role.*

of what happened. In figure 2.12 the narrator is providing background information. He states that the events he is describing happened during the winter. The narrator's eyes are directed toward an addressee as he signs DURING WINTER COLD. This is a purely textual description of the scene and no blends are used; the signer here is in the narrator role.

As the narrator continues, he demonstrates a student spitting chewing tobacco. The sequence of pictures in figure 2.13 illustrates this action. The narrator moves forward and tightens his lips as if he was spitting something. His eye gaze is not directed at an addressee as he does this and he does not produce any signs with this demonstration. This represents the narrator in the character role because he is acting as the character did.

It is commonly assumed that a narrator is either in narrator role or character role. Liddell (2003) is an exception to this generalization. He describes the simultaneous use of both surrogate and token blends with accompanying narration. Partitioning allows both textual descriptions and blends to occur simultaneously. Figure 2.14 is an example that illustrates this. The narrator is describing a school principal looking at a group of students and trying to determine which student is spitting tobacco out the window. The signer has created a surrogate blend in which his face and eye gaze blend with the face and eye gaze of the principal. This allows the

Demonstrating a person spitting.

FIGURE 2.13 *Signer in the character role.*

LOOK-AROUND$^{\cup\supset}$

FIGURE 2.14 *Signer as both narrator and character.*

addressee to directly observe the action of the |principal|. The narrator's right arm, however, is not part of the surrogate blend. If it were, it would mean that the |principal| was signing LOOK-AROUND$^{\cup\supset}$. This is clearly not the case. Instead, the signer's right hand is producing the sign LOOK-AROUND$^{\cup\supset}$. This sign provides textual description of what is happening in the blend. Is the signer in the narrator role because he produces the sign LOOK-AROUND$^{\cup\supset}$ to describe the action or in the character role because he is representing what the principal did? It is unclear how the traditional either-or terminology would describe this.

The signer remains the narrator throughout the narrative. He uses textual description to talk about what happened. The narrator in figure 2.12 signing DURING WINTER COLD, provides only textual information about the event. Figure 2.13 provides only a surrogate demonstration of what happened. The simultaneous use of a surrogate blend and textual description creates a presentation that provides a partial visual representation of the events while highlighting a part of the demonstration with the use of signs. More specifically, figure 2.14 illustrates the principal's behavior with the change in eye gaze and the facial expression of the |principal|. The sign LOOK-AROUND$^{\cup\supset}$ emphasizes the fact that the principal was scanning the room. The diagram in figure 2.15 represents the type of information presented in figures 2.12, 2.13, and 2.14. The telling of the narrative is symbolized with the rightward arrow down the center of the box. The boxes above and below this line represent the different roles used in relaying the story. The boxes above the line focus attention *on* the narrative events by demonstrating or depicting what happened. It is understood that the events have already occurred. However, the use of surrogate blends and depicting blends bring these events to the moment of telling by providing a partial visual demonstration of what happened. The boxes below the line involve textual information *about* the narrative event such as the participants and the setting.

36 : THEORETICAL BACKGROUND

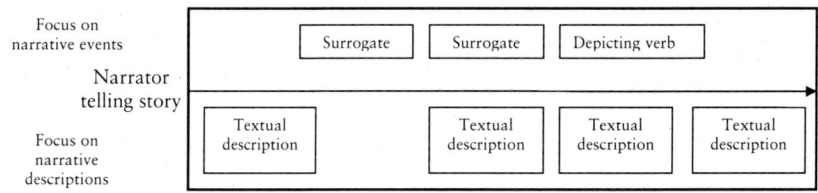

FIGURE 2.15 *Diagram representing combinations of text and real-space blending.*

Textual and Perceived Narration

In the ASL narratives I analyze I distinguish between two types of narration. I use the label *textual (T) narration* to refer to the grammatical structures the narrator uses to talk about what happened without using surrogate or depicting blends. *Perceived (P) narration* refers to the conceptual structures used when the narrator uses surrogate blends and depicting blends to demonstrate what happened. The labels distinguish the two structures to both describe them and identify when they are used. They can, and frequently do, occur simultaneously in ASL narratives.

T narration generally occurs when the signer is in narrator role. The narrator's eye gaze is primarily directed toward an addressee. Eye gaze may be momentarily shifted away from the addressee, toward one's hands for example, but during articulation of most of the signs eye gaze is toward the addressee. T narration includes the use of lexical signs to convey the information grammatically encoded by those signs; utterances in T narration do not make use of surrogate blends.

An example of T narration is provided in figure 2.16. As the narrator begins, he is turning his head from his left to his right, his eyes are closed during this transition. For the remainder of his utterance his eye gaze is directed toward the addressee on his right. The narrator uses lexical signs throughout the utterance without creating a surrogate blend or depicting blend. The result is narration that keeps the focus on the narrative event.

In contrast, P narration focuses the addressee's attention on the narrative event space, because the signer, at least partially, becomes an element of the event space through blending. The actions of the surrogate represent the actions of the blended entity at the time of the event; the result is that the past events seem part of the immediate environment. Eye gaze is also directed in a way that depicts the eye gaze of the surrogate.

An example of P narration is provided in figure 2.17. The narrator is explaining how students were ordered by the principal to open their mouths

Theoretical Background : 37

| HAVE | TWO | STUDENT | | FROM |

O-K-A-C-I-T-Y   THERE→|classroom event|

"I had two students from Oklahoma City in my class."

FIGURE 2.16 *Example of T narration.*

to prove the student was not chewing tobacco. He demonstrates what he did by opening and closing his mouth. The narrator's face represents the student's at the time of the events. The past events are partially presented in real space, which allows the addresee to "witness" the behavior that occurred.

Simultaneous Textual and Perceived Narration

As described earlier in this chapter, a blend may be partitioned so as to allow signed descriptions of activities simultaneously taking place within the blended space. Figure 2.18 provides an example of T narration combined with P narration.

The narrator is describing an incident in his classroom in which two students began to cry. The signs in figure 2.18 describe how he looked

opens mouth

FIGURE 2.17 *Example of P narration.*

38 : THEORETICAL BACKGROUND

GLANCE-UP➔|classroom event| hands forward
(up and down movement of shoulder/head recoils)
"I look up and am startled/shocked by what I see."

FIGURE 2.18 *Example of simultaneous T and P narration.*

up and was startled by seeing the students crying. In this sequence the narrator is demonstrating to the addressee his behavior at the time of the events. His face and eye gaze turn back to the area previously associated with |students| in a surrogate blend. Near the end of the sign GLANCE-UP➔|classroom event|, the signer's facial expression changes and he raises his shoulders, changes his facial expression, and his head recoils. These physical actions mark the beginning of the surrogate blend he constructs to demonstrate his internal reaction to what he saw rather than what he actually did at the time. The gesture in which his palms face outward as if pushing away something unwanted is an example of P narration. The narrator uses a surrogate blend to demonstrate what happened without the use of any lexical signs.

Signers narrate stories using T narration, P narration, and a combination of the two, allowing them to focus attention on different aspects of the narrative. Distinguishing between different types of narration allows one to describe not only the different ways signers choose to convey information, but also the ways in which these choices contribute to the addressee's experience of the narrative.

Chapter 3

Analyzing Narratives

Narratives lend themselves to analysis because they provide a "bound" unit of discourse to study. They have an identified beginning and end that mark them as separate from the surrounding discourse (Jefferson 1979; Polanyi 1985). If a narrative is told in conversation, the participants understand that the narrator will have an extended turn (Sacks, Schegloff, & Jefferson 1974). Further, personal narratives have been shown to produce more natural examples of language use (Labov 1972). This is thought to mitigate the impact of self-consciousness when individuals are recorded in the data collection process.

DATA SOURCES

I used three sources of data to analyze personal narratives. The first came from a research study of variation in ASL supported by the National Science Foundation. I videotaped Deaf ASL users from seven different areas in the United States during conversation. I analyzed three of the stories in this corpus; one produced by a white woman, recorded in Boston, Massachusetts; the second a white male recorded in Kansas City, Missouri; and the third a white male recorded in Staunton, Virginia.[1]

The second source was a 35-year-old white male who was asked by his coworkers to tell stories about his past. I recorded the narratives at his place of employment, in Silver Spring, Maryland, during a lunch hour. I analyzed five of the stories he told during the 45-minute "interview"; they describe a series of incidents that happened during a cross-country bicycle trip.

The third source of personal narratives were sociolinguistic interviews I conducted, during which I asked subjects to tell me about their past. One narrative was produced by a 26-year-old white woman and four narratives were produced by a 37-year-old Asian man. Both were recorded in Washington, D.C.; each interview lasted 60 minutes.

1. The video clips were used by permission of Ceil Lucas, the principal investigator on NSF grants SBR #9310116 and SBR #9709522. (See copyright page for figure numbers.)

SELECTING NARRATIVES

I began with 50 ASL personal narratives. Not all of these were conducive to analysis; many were eliminated because of poor video quality. To be included for analysis, the signer's hands and body had to be in the frame, the signer's face had to be clear enough to see facial expressions and eye closures, and, critically, the view of the signer had to be unobstructed. I had to eliminate those narratives produced by signers in a group setting in which another participant partially obstructed the narrator.

I was interested in data that included both male and female signers as well as people of different ages, and not necessarily those that were skilled at storytelling. The final data set consisted of 12 narratives told by two women and four men ranging in age from 24 to 75. Five of the signers were white and one was Asian.

PRODUCING TRANSCRIPTS

Once the narratives were selected I began transcribing them. It has been shown that the way in which a written transcript is produced affects the analysis of the narrative (Roberts, 1997; Bucholtz, 2000). The process of documenting a signed language on paper requires consideration, as there is no standard that captures all the necessary linguistic details. I will address these concerns in my explanation of how I transcribed the data.

Documenting Signs

As stated in chapter 1, one approach to documenting ASL signs is the use of glosses. A gloss is an English word printed in small capital letters, used to represent an ASL sign. The English word selected matches, as closely as possible, the meaning of the ASL sign. The sign produced in figure 3.1, for example, is glossed WITH. Glosses function to represent a linguistic symbol.

It is often difficult to select a word from one language to represent a linguistic symbol of another language. The sign produced by the narrator in figure 3.2 illustrates this challenge. The narrator is describing his reaction of surprise to an unexpected event. The sign and accompanying facial expression convey this concept, however English does not have a word that is the equivalent to it. One could use the gloss DAAMN! to represent this sign, but it does not convey all the meaning packaged into

FIGURE 3.1 WITH *sign*.

the ASL sign, with the accompanying facial expression and body posture. The English word comparable in meaning would require the person to pronounce the word "Daamn!" with the *a* being held longer and given extra stress at the end. Glosses provide a written way of recording a sign used in an ASL narrative, but they cannot provide enough information to interpret the true meaning of a sign.

To help readers fully understand the meaning of all the signs in a narrative, I decided to include an image of the sign along with the gloss. Although the picture in figure 3.2 does not replicate the articulation of the sign, it does enrich our understanding. The use of pictures also allows us to freeze the production of a sign to see what is happening. This draws attention to details in a signer's production that are often overlooked in real-time signing.

The inclusion of pictures in the transcript eliminates other shortcomings of transcripts produced with glosses alone. Pictures document more accurately those signs that can be directed in space and draw attention to the meanings associated with the spaces where signs are directed.

Compare the signs in figure 3.3. The signer articulates two instances of the sign THERE$^{\rightarrow L}$. In figure 3.3a, the sign THERE$^{\rightarrow L1}$ is directed ahead and to the left of the signer's body. In figure 3.3b THERE$^{\rightarrow L2}$ is directed to an area near his left shoulder. The two instances of the sign THERE$^{\rightarrow L}$ differ in that they are directed towards different locations. The narrator

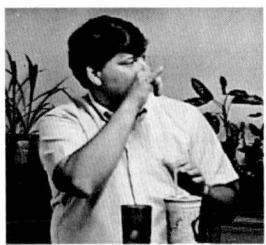

FIGURE 3.2 DAAMN! *sign*.

a. THERE→L1   b. THERE→L2

FIGURE 3.3 *Signs pointing to locations associated with the Northwest campus and Gallaudet campus.*

is introducing two different campuses into the discourse. The production of THERE→L1 locates "the Northwest campus," and THERE→L2 locates "Gallaudet University."

A few moments later the signer directs the unspecified first-person possessive sign POSS→x to the same location to which the sign THERE→L1 was directed. One can compare the articulation of these two signs in figures 3.4a and b. The dashed circle represents the area to which the signs are directed; both signs seem to be directed toward the same location in space. The narrator is describing a policy established by the administration at the Northwest campus when he articulates the sign POSS→x. Directing POSS→x toward the conceptualized location of "the Northwest Campus" identifies it as the possessor of the policy.

These two examples illustrate the limitations of using glosses alone to document the articulation of these signs. The gloss THERE for the signs in figures 3.3a and b does not express that the narrator directs the signs toward two different locations. Without this distinction, one cannot completely understand the narrative. The notational conventions introduced by Liddell (2003) mitigate this in that they allow for the indication of a

a. THERE→L1   b. POSS→x

FIGURE 3.4 *Comparison of the sign directed toward the location the Northwest campus token and a subsequent sign directed toward the same token.*

sign's direction. I have used his conventions in the glosses for figures 3.3a and b. THERE$^{\rightarrow L1}$ represents the articulation in which the narrator directs the sign ahead and to the left of the signer's body. The superscript →L1 indicates that the sign is directed toward a location L1. The superscript →L2 indicates that this articulation of THERE is directed toward a different location, L2.

The use of this system, however, does not always allow one to see when signs may be directed at the same locations. In figures 3.4a and b, the narrator directs the signs THERE$^{\rightarrow L1}$ and POSS$^{\rightarrow x}$ toward the same area. The arrow identifies that the signs are directed in space, but it is not clear that they are directed toward the same location. We must see where the sign is directed in order to understand the sign's meaning. Signs are frequently directed in the signing space when token and surrogate blends are used. It is critical that a transcript convey where a sign is directed in order for the sign to be interpreted correctly..

The spatial variability of depicting verbs provides another reason for the use of pictures in a transcript. These are verbs which, in addition to encoding meaning about an action or state, also depict a certain aspect of their meaning. For example, the narrator in figure 3.5a produces the sign LINE-OF-PEOPLE-WALKING-ALONG$^{\downarrow L1\text{-}L2}$ to describe a single-file line of people walking casually. In the video one can see the signer's fingers wiggling while he moves his hands forward. His facial expression provides information on the type of movement the depicting verb represents, which was casual or unhurried. The movement of the hands forward conveys

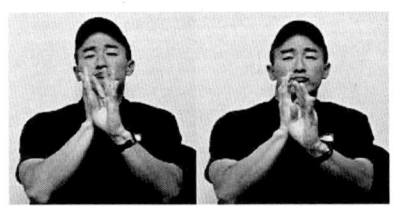

a. LINE-OF-PEOPLE-WALKING-ALONG$^{\downarrow L1\text{-}L2}$

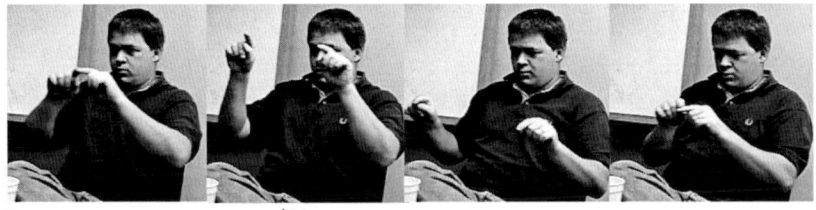

b. SQUARE-SHAPED-OBJECT$^{\downarrow L1}$

FIGURE 3.5 *Depicting verbs represented with gloss and image.*

the direction the people moved. The position of the hands depicts how the people were lined up one behind the other. The gloss assigned to this sign, LINE-OF-PEOPLE-WALKING-ALONG$^{\downarrow L1\text{-}L2}$, provides information to the reader that the people were in a line and walking. The superscript ↓L1-L2 identifies that there was movement between two locations. However, the gloss does not provide the information that the narrator's facial expression contributes: the direction the people walked and casual manner in which they walked. Similarly, in figure 3.5b, the gloss SQUARE-SHAPED-OBJECT$^{\downarrow L1}$ does not identify the size of the square-shaped object. The narrator is using the sign to describe a piece of paper, and the way in which he articulates the sign represents the approximate size of the paper. If the paper were poster size, he would have extended his arms higher and wider. The size contributes to the meaning of the sign, and this information is most easily available if pictures are included.

These examples illustrate the need for pictures to accompany glosses, and for glosses to be written with the notation convention that marks placement and direction. They demonstrate how the addressee draws on not only the articulation of the sign, but also the narrator's body position, eye gaze, and facial expression in order to comprehend meaning. Further evidence of the significance of body position, eye gaze, and facial expression comes when the narrator relies only on these to convey meaning. The examples in figure 3.6 illustrate this.

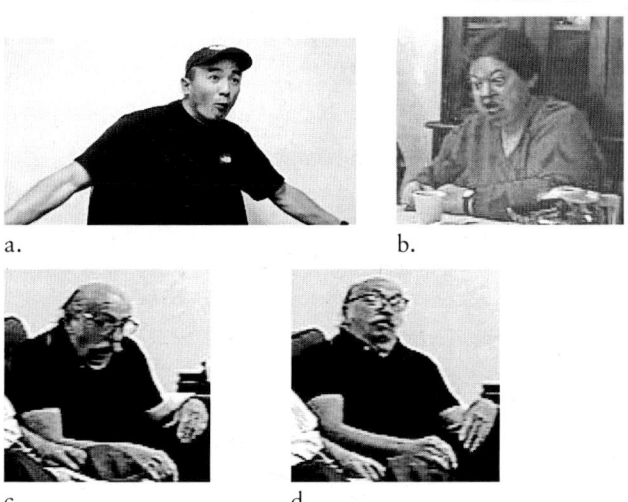

FIGURE 3.6 *Facial expressions and body postures without accompanying lexical signs.*

It would be difficult to gloss what the narrators are signing in these examples because they are not producing any lexical signs. However, through facial expression and body posture, the narrators are conveying information that is significant to one's understanding of the narrative. To describe each expression as a "surprised look" is insufficient; although this is an accurate description of the facial expression, it omits how the body is positioned and where the eye gaze is directed. The expressions in figures 3.6c and d could be described as "surprised," but in 3.6c the narrator is directing his eye gaze downward, hunching his shoulders slightly forward, and opening his mouth. In 3.6d the narrator is directing his eye gaze upward, pulling his shoulders back, and closing his mouth. The direction of the eye gaze and body position differ because he is reacting to events associated with different areas in the signing space. The eye gazes and body positions provide the information necessary to access the correct space in ways that lexical signs cannot.

Chapter 2 described how eye gaze and body position assist in the identification of T and P narration; therefore, these features must also be incorporated into the transcript. Figure 3.7a illustrates the narrator using T narration and Figure 3.7b his use of T and P narration. These utterances occur in succession and demonstrate how the change in narration type is indicated by a change in eye gaze, body position, and facial expression.

a. THINK   ENOUGH   TIME
"I thought enough time had elapsed."

b. GLANCE-UP→lclassroom eventl   hands forward
(up and down movement of shoulder/head recoils)

"I look up and am startled/shocked by what I see."

FIGURE 3.7 *Use of T and P narration.*

During the T narration the narrator signs THINK ENOUGH TIME while directing his eye gaze toward the addressee seated to his left. As he produces the sign GLANCE-UP→|classroom event|, he directs his eye gaze downward and then up as he articulates the sign. He then directs his eye gaze toward the space in front of him. His head and shoulders recoil as if reacting to what he "sees" ahead of him. This second utterance is produced using both T and P narration. It is impossible to rely on a gloss to convey what is happening with the eyes, face, and body. A visual representation is needed to identify what the signer produces.

ASL narrators often convey information with the use of gestures or a demonstration of action rather than lexical signs. Figure 3.8 illustrates three such instances. Figures 3.8a and b illustrate how a signer describes an action through demonstration. In figure 3.8a the narrator explains how he was asked to open his mouth to show that he was not chewing tobacco. The narrator simply demonstrates what he did. The narrator in figure 3.8b

a. opens and closes mouth

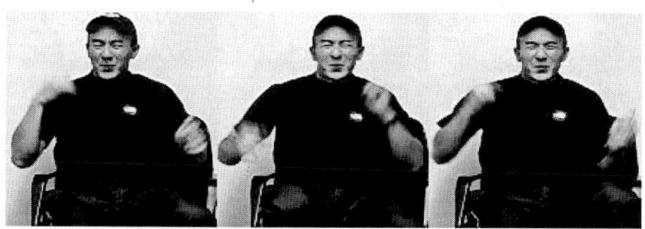

b. demonstration of running

c. shrug

FIGURE 3.8 *Use of demonstrations or gestures without lexical signs.*

Analyzing Narratives : 47

is describing his experience competing in a biathlon. He demonstrates how he ran, pumping his arms up and down as if actually running. In the final example, figure 3.8c, the signer simply shrugs to describe a character's reaction to a situation. Although these narrators do not produce ASL signs, the demonstrations and gestures they produce are integral to the narrative.

Transcript Conventions

The Appendix contains keys to the enhanced glossing conventions used in this book. To further assist readers in understanding the examples, I merged the glossing conventions with the images. For signs that did not involve two or more locations, a single image represents the sign with the gloss written below. However, many signs require more than one location to produce the sign; these signs are represented by two or more images. These images are placed next to each other with no space between them and the gloss centered underneath the images. Figures 3.9a and b illustrate these two types of basic signs and how they are documented. A time code was used to mark the beginning of each "line." When possible, pictures of all the signs produced for a single utterance appear on the same line. The length of some utterances prevents this, so they may continue on the line below.

FINGERSPELLING

I divided the fingerspelling that occurred in the narratives I examined into two broad categories, *careful fingerspelling* and *lexicalized fingerspelling*. For instances of careful fingerspelling, I included an image of each letter articulated and provide the word underneath with hyphens between each letter. In a few cases I only provided the first and last letter of the carefully fingerspelled word, due to space limitations. For lexicalized

a. VOLUNTEER   b. DEAF

FIGURE 3.9 *Comparison of transcription of a sign with one location and a sign with more than one location.*

a. O-R-E-G-O-N

b. #THEN

FIGURE 3.10 *Documentation of careful and lexicalized fingerspelling.*

fingerspelling I provided two stills which represent the initial and final hand configuration and position. The symbol # appears before the gloss of lexicalized fingerspelling. Each letter of the corresponding English word is present in the gloss regardless of whether a sign for that letter is part of the sign. Examples are provided in figures 3.10a and b.

SIGNS THAT CAN BE DIRECTED

Several signs in this category have been used in earlier examples (THERE→L1, POSS→x, GLANCE-UP→|classroom event|). Other signs that are representative of this category are signs that can indicate different referents depending on initial and final location, such as GIVE→x. Signs can also be directed in different ways as they are articulated. Figure 3.11 illustrates an example of a sign that can be directed.

DEPICTING VERBS

Depicting verbs typically require multiple images to capture their multiple different parts. Recall that there are three different types of depicting

LOOK-AROUND ᓂ|students|

FIGURE 3.11 *Example documentation of a sign that can be directed.*

RECTANGULAR-CONTAINER-EXTENDED-TO^{L1-L2}

a. LONG-ENTITY-BE-AT$^{\downarrow L}$
fragment buoy (of RECTANGULAR-CONTAINER-EXTENDED-TO^{L1-L2})

b. FLAT-BROAD-SURFACE-EXTEND-TO$^{\downarrow L1-L2}$

c. VEHICLE-DRIVE-TO$^{\downarrow L1-L2}$
BROAD-SURFACE$^{\downarrow L1}$

FIGURE 3.12 *Gloss of depicting verbs.*

verbs. I reproduce examples from chapter 2 here to illustrate how these signs are glossed. I use more than one image to attempt to capture the articulation of these signs. For example, in the articulation of the sign RECTANGULAR-CONTAINER-EXTENDED-TO$^{\downarrow L1-L2}$ (figure 3.12a), three different images show how the signer demonstrated the shape of the container he described. Similarly, figure 3.12c uses three images to show the direction and distance moved in the signing space.

Defining a Line

Narratives are not produced in a continuous, uninterrupted flow but in spurts. Chafe (1994) has discussed the spurt-like nature of narratives. He relates the way people start and stop to the jerky way human consciousness scans the information banks of memory. Each time a narrator focuses on an idea, a burst of talk results, surrounded by very brief pauses. These bursts of "idea units" often consist of a single phrase or clause and end with a slight rise or fall in intonation. Each expresses what can roughly be seen as a new concept. In the narratives Chafe studied, idea units tend to be about two seconds or six words long. The practice now is to have the transcript reflect how the speaker broke the words into units, or utterances.

I apply this philosophy to the ASL narratives. A "line" in my transcripts is equivalent to an idea unit. As with spoken narratives, brief pauses (.20 seconds, using the time code from QuickTime) occur between the lines.

ANALYSIS

The analysis was initiated by the production of the transcripts. Once the transcript was produced I looked at each line and attempted to describe its function. I also noted how the information was being conveyed. I identified any use of textual narration, surrogates, depicting verbs, tokens, buoys, or any combination of these.

For example, the line in figure 3.13 has three functions. The first is to link the signer's narrative to the conversation that he has been a participant in. The signer signs PRO-1 THINK, which is similar to the English "It makes me think of," to signal to the addressee that his narrative is relevant to the preceding discussion. Next, he identifies participants in the

"It makes me think of my class."

FIGURE 3.13 *Identifying the use of grammatical structures.*

narrative with the articulation of POSS-1 CLASS THERE→|classroom event|. The use of the possessive pronoun identifies the narrator as one participant in the event. Finally, to identify where the event occurred he signs CLASS THERE→|classroom event|. He associates the concept of a classroom with the area near his left shoulder resulting in the creation of a token blend by directing THERE→|classroom event| toward the token |classroom event|. The narrator conveys these three pieces of information using textual descriptions, PRO-1 THINK POSS-1 CLASS THERE→|classroom event|, while also making use of a token blend.

A line can convey more than one type of meaning. A summary of the categories of meaning conveyed in the 12 narratives analyzed will be discussed in chapter 8.

In the narratives I analyzed, I noticed moments when the narrative seemed to pause and after those pauses conveyed a different type of information. Four behaviors clustered at these moments: an extended eye closure, a head nod, lowering of the hands, and a pause in signing. Two grammatical structures frequently occurred immediately after the behaviors. One was a lexical sign such as THEN, ANYWAY, or NEXT, and the other was the use of topicalization to mark the first sign of the subsequent line. Previous analysis of ASL narratives (Gee and Kegl 1983, Bahan and Supalla 1995) had described similar breaks in the flow of a narrative so I measured the length of eye blinks and pauses in signing. I used the time code in QuickTime to measure the duration of the eye closings and pauses. The presence of a head nod and whether or not the hands were lowered was noted. A narrator closed his or her eyes for an average of .45 of a second at the end of a section. In contrast, the average length of an eye closure at other points in a narrative based on a random sampling was .2 of a second. All four behaviors did not always appear, but they consistently clustered together across all narratives. The grammatical structures were also not always used, but did consistently appear after the four behaviors.

I documented where these breaks occurred on the transcripts. I also marked these breaks on the tables listing the function of each line. The information conveyed in each resulting section was of a similar type, which I then grouped it into six broad categories: introduction, background, main event, explication, reflection and conclusion. In the following chapters I will describe each of these sections of a narrative in more detail, and in chapter 8 I will summarize the type and frequency of structures used.

Chapter 4

A Prototypical Narrative

Each of the narratives I examined can each be divided into six sections: introduction, background, main event, explication, reflection, and conclusion. The *main events* section is comprised of a series of events plus elaborations. The elaborations provide additional detail to the story. The remainder of this chapter uses the narrative "Moment of Silence" to illustrate the sections of a narrative and to explain how divisions were made.

Moment of Silence
That makes me think of something that happened in my classroom. I was teaching at an interpreter training program. I had two students in my class who were from Oklahoma City. Exactly one week, the week after the bombing, an announcement was made that there would be a minute-long moment of silence at 9 o'clock. This is fine with me. This would be during my class which met from 8 to 10, which was fine with me. At the designated time we all got up and stood quietly in a circle. After about a minute I opened my eyes. I thought enough time had elapsed. I look up and am startled by what I see. Daamn, the two students from Oklahoma City were crying. I looked at them and thought, "Wow." I was moved by it. I found out that several of their friends had died in the bombing. So, they knew some people there. As I was looking at this I thought, "Wow, I wonder what that is like?" The experience really touched me.

INTRODUCTORY SECTION

The introduction serves two purposes, to secure the floor or mark the beginning of a new story and to introduce the subject of the narrative. In the narratives I examined, the signers take four steps to introduce the narrative's subject: they identify the topic of the story, introduce the participants, identify the location, and foreshadow events to come. In the "Moment of Silence" narrative, which is told in a group setting, the narrator has to secure the floor before he begins his narrative. The conversation preceding this narrative revolved around the Oklahoma City bombing at the Alfred P. Murrah Federal Building in April 1995. The narrator secures the floor by linking his story to the one that has just been told by the man seated to his left. Figures 4.1a and b illustrate how the narrator connects his story with the one that was just told. The signer first signs AWFUL, "That would be awful." This is his comment on the preceding signer's comment. He directs his eye gaze toward the previous narrator and signs PRO-1 THINK POSS-1 CLASS THERE→|classroom event|, "It makes me think of my class." This comment links the story he will tell with what has just been discussed.

Once he has secured the floor, he continues his introduction by identifying the topic of the narrative, the participants, and the location where the events took place. This information is provided by the signing illustrated in figure 4.1b–d. The signer's eye gaze is alternatively directed toward two of his addressees throughout the introduction. Maintaining eye contact with an addressee is typical of periods of T narration. In figure 4.1b and c the signer is looking toward the addressee on his left. While his eye gaze is to his left, he signs PRO-1 THINK POSS CLASS THERE→|classroom event|, "It makes me think of my class," and then PRO-1 TEACH INTERPRET TRAINING PROGRAM THERE→|classroom event|, "I taught at an interpreter training program

a. AWFUL
   That would be awful.

b. PRO-1   THINK   POSS-1

           CLASS   THERE→|classroom event|

"That makes me think of something that happened in my classroom."
FIGURE 4.1 *Introductory section.*

there." These two lines along with the addressees' background knowledge identify the topic and location of the event that took place in a classroom. The signer, for example, never uses the sign CLASSROOM. Based on one's experience with where teaching typically takes place, it would be natural to assume that a classroom would be the location for the story.

The signer next directs his eye gaze toward an addressee seated to his right and produces the signs in figure 4.1d: HAVE TWO STUDENT FROM O-K-A-C-I-T-Y THERE→|classroom event|, "I had two students from Oklahoma City in my class." The signer mentions two students who will be central participants in the main-events section.

The sign THERE→|classroom event| is produced by the signer three times. The initial production associates a particular area in space with the class that he teaches. The narrator thus creates a token blend, which is a common

c. PRO-1   TEACH   INTERPRET   TRAINING   PROGRAM

THERE→|classroom event|
"I was teaching at an interpreter training program."

d. HAVE   TWO   STUDENT   FROM

O-K-A-C-I-T-Y   THERE→|classroom event|
"I had two students in my class from Oklahoma City."

FIGURE 4.1 *continued*

A Prototypical Narrative : 55

| THERE→|classroom event| | THERE→|classroom event| | THERE→|classroom event| |
| My class. | My interpreter training class. | My interpreter training class with two students from Oklahoma City in it. |

FIGURE 4.2 *Example of* THERE$^{→L}$ *directed toward the token* |classroom event|.

feature of ASL narrative introductions. The second articulation ends the string of signs in 4.1c, thereby associating the content with the |classroom event| that the token THERE→|classroom event| is directed toward. Similarly, the final instance of THERE→|classroom event| associates the content of the signing in figure 4.1d with the same token. By directing THERE→|classroom event| toward the same token following each string of signs, the signer associates all the content of figures 4.1b–d with the |classroom event|. Figure 4.2 compares these three instances, with a circle marking the location of the token |classroom event|. This token will be important later in the narrative, when the signer describes the main events. He will direct his eye gaze at this same general direction when he adds surrogate demonstrations to the narrative.

The primary functions of the introduction are to secure the floor, mark the beginning of a new story, identify the topic, and identify the participants and/or the location—although not all functions are accomplished in every introduction. In this narrative the signer secures the floor and connects the story to the topic the group has been discussing, the Oklahoma City bombing. In figure 4.1 the narrator identifies the location of the story and the participants. As is typical of periods of T narration, he directs his gaze toward one or the other of the addressees throughout the introduction. The signer marks the end of the introduction by closing his eyes briefly and relaxing his hands.

BACKGROUND SECTION

The background section's primary function is to orient the addressee. This includes providing basic information such as topic, participants, and location. This might be the initial mention of location or, if the location has already been mentioned in the introduction, the background section comprises additional information about the location. The background section also provides specific information necessary for comprehending the main event. This information is conveyed through a series of alternations between T narration and P narration, which can include depicting blends, surrogate blends (demonstrations), and token blends.

The introduction to the "Moment of Silence" narrative provides information about the topic (an event in the classroom), the participants (two students from Oklahoma City), and a location (the classroom). The background section elaborates further by providing specifics about the event. This information is needed to understand what will happen in the main-events section of the narrative. The background section is illustrated in figure 4.3.

The narrator begins his background section by identifying when the event occurred. Figures 4.3a and b illustrate this sequence. With the exception of the initial sign, the signer directs his face and eye gaze toward one addressee—typical of periods of T narration. The signer continues by explaining that an announcement was made that a moment of silence would be observed. This is illustrated in figure 4.3c, ANNOUNCE HAVE TIME 9 O'CLOCK (Pause) QUIET FOR {ONE}{MINUTE}, "An announcement was made that there would be a minute-long moment of silence at 9 o'clock."

In figure 4.3d the signer switches for the first time to P narration. During FINE his face and eye gaze are no longer directed at an addressee. He appears to be providing constructed dialogue involving his thoughts, "This is fine with me." Similarly, the signs FINE in figure 4.3f and figure 4.3h also appear to show the signer's thoughts about the announcements. Support for the assumption that this is P narration is that the narrator provides a surrogate expression of his thoughts by directing his face and eye gaze away from all of his addressees.

In figures 4.3e and g the narrator provides additional information about the main event. First he explains that this event will occur in the middle of his class time, DURING POSS-1 CLASS TIME EIGHT TO TEN, "This would be during my class, which met from 8 to 10." Then he describes the motivation for the event, PRO$^{\rightarrow |classroom\ event|}$ WANT HONOR$^{\cup \rightarrow \Sigma \rightarrow}$, "The intention was to honor the victims." He directs his face and eye gaze toward the addressees throughout the production of these signs with two exceptions. The first occurs when he produces EIGHT TO. During these two signs he directs his eye gaze toward his hands. This could be T narration with eye

A Prototypical Narrative : 57

gaze used to emphasize the time frame, or it could be T narration with the addition of P narration: the horizontal trajectory of his hands creates a metaphorical real-space blend, using space to show a span of time. Since he makes no subsequent reference to this space, I will leave the choice between these two alternatives open. The narrator also directs his face

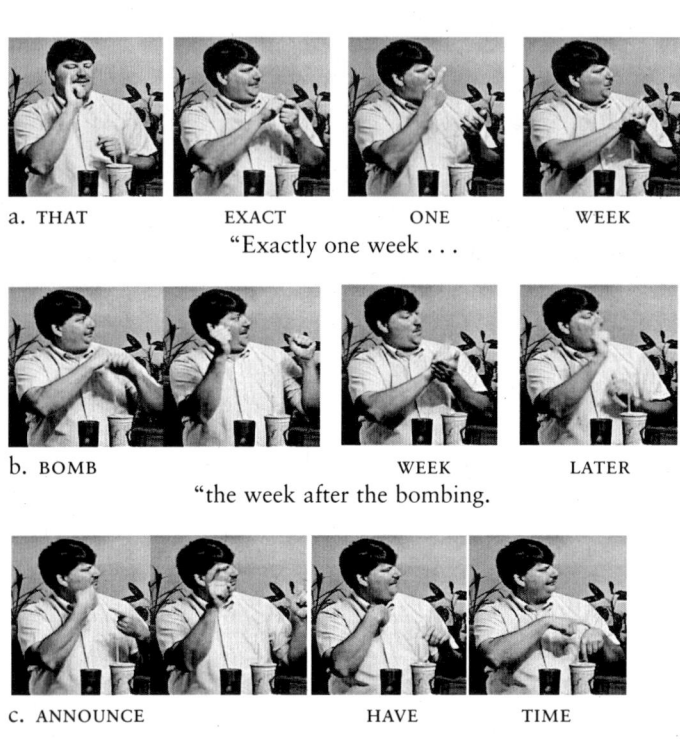

a. THAT EXACT ONE WEEK
"Exactly one week . . .

b. BOMB WEEK LATER
"the week after the bombing.

c. ANNOUNCE HAVE TIME

9 O'CLOCK (Pause) QUIET

FOR {ONE} {MINUTE}
"an announcement was made that there would be a minute-long moment of silence at 9 o'clock."

FIGURE 4.3 *Background section.*

d. "FINE"
   "This is fine with me."

e. DURING   POSS-1   CLASS   TIME

   EIGHT   TO   TEN
   "This would be during my class which met from 8 to 10."

f. "FINE"
   "This is fine with me."

  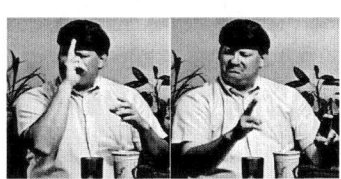

g. PRO→|classroom event| WANT   HONOR↻→Σ→
   "The intention was to honor the victims."

h. "FINE"   FINE"
   "This is fine with me."

FIGURE 4.3 *continued*

and gaze away from an addressee when he produces PRO→|classroom event| WANT—he directs his face and eye gaze toward the area associated with the classroom. Directing PRO→|classroom event| toward the token |classroom event| does not provide evidence that this is also a period of P narration. Although directing his face and eye gaze in this way draws additional attention to |classroom event|, the narrator is still just talking about the event.

This narrator has provided background information that will be useful in comprehending the main event. He has identified the topic of the main event as the observation of a moment of silence in honor of the Oklahoma City bombing victims. He has specified the time this would happen, mentioning that it coincided with when his class met. The signer ends this section by briefly closing his eyes and relaxing his hands.

MAIN-EVENTS SECTION

The main-events section describes the events that occur in the narrative. It also includes elaborations that expand on those events. In general, events are described in the order in which they occur and elaborations provide the details that flesh out those events. The details are generally related to one or more of the following categories: physical movement, description of objects, reaction, constructed dialogue, supplemental information, and participant/setting information. Typically this section consists of a complex mixture of T narration and P narration.

In "Moment of Silence," the main-events section consists of the narrator's description of three events. He elaborates on each one after it is introduced. In describing the first narrative event he states that everyone stood for the moment of silence. He elaborates this with a surrogate blend in which he demonstrates his actions during this event. The narrator describes the second narrative event by stating that he opened his eyes. He elaborates on this event by explaining why he opened his eyes. He follows this by demonstrating through a surrogate blend how he reacted to what he saw when he opened his eyes. He describes the final event with a statement that he saw the two girls crying when he opened his eyes. He then demonstrates himself looking at the students and describes how he felt at that moment. The signer alternates between periods of T narration and periods of P narration to tell this story; he uses T narration to state what happened and P narration to elaborate those events.

Narrative Event #1:

STAND-UP   STAND-IN-CIRCLE*

QUIET
"[At the designated time we all] got up
and stood quietly in a circle."

Elaboration 1A:

STAND   QUIET
"[So we are] standing there."   "It is quiet."

*I consider the sign STAND-IN-CIRCLE a lexical sign, not one that depicts the action. It is similar to STAND-UP, which does not describe exactly how a person stands up.

FIGURE 4.4 *Main event #1 with elaboration.*

Figure 4.4 illustrates the narrator's description of a main event with an elaboration. He describes a group of people getting up and standing for a moment of silence with the lexical signs STAND-UP STAND-IN-CIRCLE QUIET, "[We all] got up and stood quietly in a circle." During these signs the signer directs his face and eye gaze toward his addressees, typical of periods of T narration. In elaboration 1A, the signer's eye gaze turns toward an area associated with the students and classroom and he appears to adopt a posture consistent with a bowed head. These two changes suggest that he has created a surrogate blend in which his head demonstrates (gives a physical presence to) what he was doing at that time. He creates the surrogate blend and repeats the sign QUIET. Figure 4.5 illustrates the differences in eye gaze and posture for the two instances of QUIET. Through the use of the surrogate blend he demonstrates what he did in the classroom during

QUIET	QUIET
"It was quiet."	"[So here I am with my head bowed]."
	"It is quiet."

FIGURE 4.5 *Two instances of* QUIET.

the moment of silence. This allows the addressee to see a blended instance of a portion of the event. This blended instance is limited in this case to showing that his head was bowed. Although limited by the partitioning of the blend, this is nevertheless new information. The signer has made no previous mention of bowed heads in introducing this episode.

The repetition of the sign QUIET is further evidence that the second line is an elaboration of narrative event #1. It ties the surrogate blend to the previous narration. The second instance of QUIET does not mark a new event; rather, it elaborates on what he previously described. By mentioning that the room was quiet while simultaneously presenting the surrogate blend, the signer links the blend to the situation previously described.

Eye-gaze change and the repetition of QUIET are not the only markers that the signer has transitioned from T narration of the event to T and P narration that includes a surrogate blend. There is also a difference in the facial expression during the production of the two instances of QUIET. Figure 4.6 illustrates the differences in head position and facial expressions used in these two instances of QUIET. During the articulation of QUIET in figure 4.6a, the mouth forms a straight line across the signer's face, which gives the impression of information being stated in a matter of fact manner. In figure 4.6b the mouth is turned downward, almost as

a. Main event: QUIET   b. Elaboration: QUIET

FIGURE 4.6 *Comparison of facial expression while producing* QUIET.

in a frown. This second expression is consistent with the mood created by the "bowed head" demonstration. The repetition of QUIET combined with face and eye gaze directed away from an addressee, bowed head, and facial expression all assist in identifying the surrogate blend in the elaboration of the narrative event.

Figure 4.7a shows how the signer signs the second event. He signs #THEN {ONE}{MINUTE} OPEN-EYES, "After about a minute I opened my

Narrative Event #2:

a. #THEN   {ONE} {MINUTE}

OPEN-EYES
"After about a minute I opened my eyes."

Elaboration 2A:

b. THINK   ENOUGH   TIME
"I thought enough time had elapsed."

Elaboration 2B:

c. GLANCE-UP→|classroom event| hands forward
(up and down movement of shoulder/head recoils)
"I look up and am startled/shocked by what I see."

FIGURE 4.7 *Main event #2 with elaborations.*

A Prototypical Narrative : 63

eyes." As with narrative event #1, the signer only uses T narration to state what happened while directing his face and eye gaze toward the addressee. The use of the sign #THEN marks what follows as the next event in sequence. The elaboration in figure 4.7b, THINK ENOUGH TIME, "I thought enough time had elapsed," explains why he chose to open his eyes. The reason for what happened in narrative event #2 is provided in this elaboration. This information is not critical to understanding the narrative; rather, it provides another detail to the story. Elaborations allow the narrator a means of enhancing his narrative. His face and eye gaze remain directed toward the addressee on his left as this period of T narration continues.

In figure 4.7c his face and eye gaze turn back to the area associated with the students and classroom, signifying a return to the previous surrogate blend. He signs GLANCE-UP$^{\rightarrow |classroom\ event|}$ (up and down movement of shoulder/head recoils) and then produces a gesture in which his hands are raised in front of him. I interpret the "recoil" gesture as expressing both his surprise and discomfort. An English translation of the gesture might be something like, "I look up and am startled/shocked by what I see." He signs GLANCE-UP$^{\rightarrow |classroom\ event|}$ to explain what he did. This simultaneous T narration and P narration explains what the narrator did as well as partially demonstrates the behavior. Near the end of the sign GLANCE-UP$^{\rightarrow |classroom\ event|}$, the signer's facial expression changes and he raises his shoulders, changes his facial expression, and recoils the head as illustrated in figure 4.8. These physical actions mark the beginning of the surrogate blend used to demonstrate his internal reaction to what he saw rather than what he actually did physically at the time. The blend continues as he produces a gesture that looks as if he is pushing something that is unwanted away from him. This surrogate blend makes explicit his thoughts and feelings about what happened at the time he opened his eyes. This gesture is an example of P narration.

Relaxed expression   Tense expression

FIGURE 4.8 *Expression change.*

Narrative Event #3:

a. DAAMN!   STUDENT   CRY[DURATIONAL]
"Daamn, the students from Oklahoma City were crying."

Elaboration 3A:

b. LOOK-AT→|classroom event| WOW
"I looked at the students and thought, 'Wow.'"

Elaboration 3B:

c. TOUCH-HEART
"I was moved by it."

FIGURE 4.9 *Main event #3 with elaborations.*

Figure 4.9 illustrates his signing of the third and final main event. In figure 4.9a he explains why he was startled when he signs DAAMN! STUDENT CRY[DURATIONAL], "Daamn, the students were crying." Again, since the signer is using T narration, he maintains eye contact with the addressee. In figure 4.9b the signer creates a surrogate blend to demonstrate how he reacted to the students crying. He directs his eye gaze to the surrogate |classroom event| as he narrates with the sign LOOK-AT→|classroom event| WOW, "I am looking at the students and, 'Wow'." His eye gaze and facial expression provide the clues that he has created a surrogate blend. Although his eye gaze remains focused on the |classroom event| during the production of these signs, his facial expression changes. Figure 4.10 illustrates the two different expressions. The expression that accompanies LOOK-AT→|classroom event| expresses his feelings at that time. Although it is not visible in figure 4.9a,

a. Facial expression accompanying LOOK-AT→|classroom event|

b. Facial expression accompanying WOW

FIGURE 4.10 *Two different facial expressions.*

the signer actually pulls his head backwards as well. This is similar to what he did during the surrogate demonstration in figure 4.9b. His facial expression and body movement in the surrogate blend convey how he reacted at the time. This example of narration illustrates how two types of information can be simultaneously expressed using T and P narration. He signs LOOK-AT→|classroom event|, which describes his activity of looking at the students. His facial expression and slight recoil then provide information about his emotional reaction to what he saw. The sign WOW is also complemented by his facial expression; describing his further reaction to seeing the students cry, his rounded lips create an expression that conveys intensity.

In elaboration 3B, the narrator continues to expand on his reaction to seeing the students cry, using T narration. Although it is difficult to see in the picture, the signer's face and eye gaze are once again directed toward the addressee on his left. This change in face and eye gaze away from the area associated with the classroom indicates that the surrogate blend used in Elaboration 3A is no longer in use. In figure 4.9c the signer comments on the event with the sign TOUCH-HEART, "I was moved by it." An enlarged frame of the signer producing TOUCH-HEART is provided in figure 4.11. His lips maintain the shape that accompanied WOW. The simultaneous use of the sign TOUCH-HEART and a facial expression convey his feeling about what he experienced. The sign TOUCH-HEART explicitly identifies how the experience affected him. His expression complements the lexical sign.

Elaboration 3B concludes the main events section of the narrative. As with previous sections, there is an eye closure after the final sign. The narrator does not introduce any new episodes after this.

TOUCH-HEART

FIGURE 4.11 *T narration used to expression reaction to the experience.*

EXPLICATION SECTION

In the explication section, the narrator clarifies or expounds on one of the narrative events, providing additional details. In the narratives I examined, signers typically alternated between T narration, P narration, and the simultaneous use of both to convey the explication, with P narration including depiction or surrogate demonstrations. Figure 4.12 illustrates how this is accomplished in the "Moment of Silence" narrative.

In the explication section of this narrative, the narrator explains why the students were crying. He states that he found out the two students from Oklahoma City had several friends that had died in the bombing. He signs DET→x FIND POSS→x SEVERAL FRIEND DIE THERE→y SAME, "I found out that several of their friends had died in the bombing" (figure 4.12a). He directs his face and eye gaze toward one of the addressees throughout this sequence, typical of periods of T narration. He continues in figure 4.12b by signing #SO PRO→x KNOW SOME PEOPLE THERE→y, "So, they knew some people there." This statement does not seem necessary since this information follows from the sequence in figure 4.12a. He most likely makes this statement because it is the point of the story: these students had a connection to the events of Oklahoma City. The signer's eye gaze is directed toward the space associated with the students from Oklahoma, but he is not describing what happened. He is conveying information about the people associated with the space that his eye gaze is directed toward. This section concludes with a brief eye closure.

REFLECTION SECTION

In the reflection section the narrator comments on how he or she felt about what happened in the main events. The signer reinforces his feeling

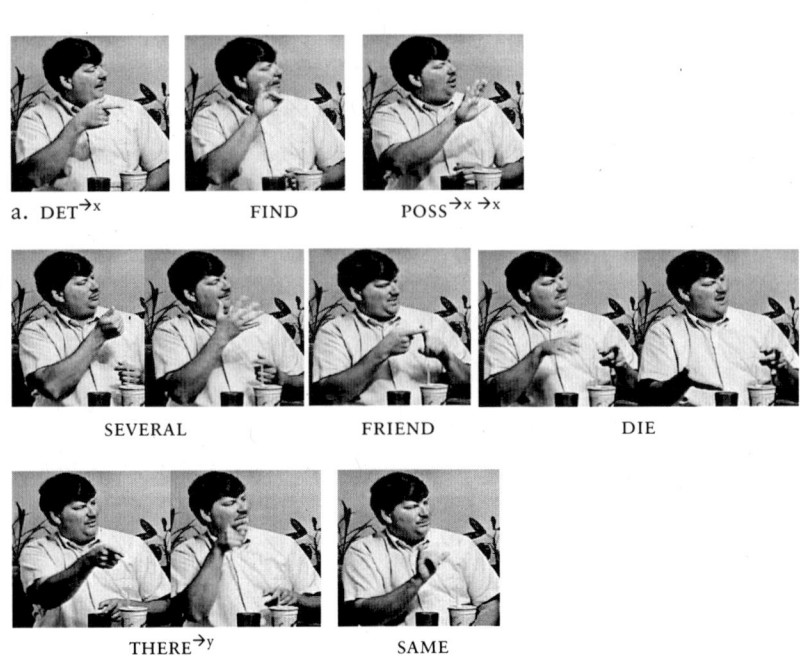

a. DET→x   FIND   POSS→x →x

SEVERAL   FRIEND   DIE

THERE→y   SAME

"I found out that several of their friends had died in the bombing."

b. #SO   PRO→x   KNOW

SOME   PEOPLE   THERE→

"So, they knew some people there."

FIGURE 4.12 *Explication section.*

of being overwhelmed and touched by what he witnessed. In figure 4.13a he directs his eye gaze toward the |classroom event| with the students and signs WOW LOOK-AT→|classroom event| WONDER, "As I was looking at this I thought, 'Wow, I wonder what that is like.'" He provides P narration using the signs WOW, LOOK-AT→|classroom event| and WONDER with a thoughtful expression. He concludes the reflection section in figure 4.13b by direct-

a. WOW LOOK-AT→|classroom event| WONDER

"As I was looking at this I thought, 'Wow, I wonder what that is like.'"

b. TOUCH-HEART   WOW

"That experience really touched me."

c. lowered hands

FIGURE 4.13 *Reflection.*

ing his face and eye gaze first to the addressee on his right then to the addressee on his left while signing TOUCH-HEART WOW, "That experience really touched me." At the conclusion of these signs he closes his eyes briefly and lowers his hand to his lap.

CLOSING SECTION

The function of the closing section is to mark the end of the narrative and relinquish the floor. The signer in this narrative accomplishes this by putting his arms down and directing his eye gaze toward the person sitting to his left to watch what he signs (figure 4.13c).

Chapter 5

The Structure of Introduction

and Background Sections

in ASL Narratives

All of the narratives in this study contain at least an introduction, a main event, and a conclusion. Some also contain background information, explanation, or elaboration of the main event, or reflections on the main event. Therefore, I have divided the narratives into two parts, which I have labeled *introduction* and *background*. These two sections are grouped together because they serve the overall function of orienting the listener to the story that will be told.

GENERAL CHARACTERISTICS OF INTRODUCTIONS

A narrative's introduction first either secures the floor or identifies the start of a new story, depending on whether the narrative is told in a group setting or to a single addressee. The introduction then provides up to four types of information: identification of the topic of the story, introduction of the participants, identification of the location, and foreshadowing of the events to come. Table 5.1 lists all the narratives I analyzed and charts those of the six functions that are included in each introduction. No story conveys all possible types of information in the introduction, but every story accomplishes at least two of the six possible functions.

Of the six sections in the narratives, the introductions and conclusions are the most uniform. The average length of time given to the entire introductory section is 4.3 seconds. The shortest introduction lasts only 1 second and the lengthiest continues for 10 seconds. The introductions average 2.75 lines and vary from a single line in three narratives to 5 lines in two others. In all the narratives taken from face-to-face interviews, the narrator always initially makes eye contact with the interlocutor. In the

TABLE 5.1. *Elements of Introductions.*

Story	Get Floor	Mark New Story	ID Topic	ID Participants	ID Location	Fore-shadow
Conversations						
Card Game	X		X	X		
Moment of Silence	X		X	X	X	
Tobacco Story	X			X		
1 on 1						
Around the World		X			X	
Biathlon		X	X	X		X
Biking Over Water		X			X	
Cheerleading		X	X			
East Coast Beaches		X	X			
Firehouse Fun		X	X		X	
Flat Tires		X		X		
Junior Year Football		X	X	X		X
Left Behind		X				X

narratives that occur in a group setting, two narrators make eye contact with a single person and one narrator scans the group. At the end of each introduction section the narrator blinks. The average length of time the eyes remain closed is .41 seconds, ranging from .17 to .60 seconds. These eye closures are accompanied by head nods in seven of the introductions. In two of the three conversation introductions the eye closures occur during head turns in which the narrator changes whom he or she is looking at.

FUNCTION OF INTRODUCTIONS

The introduction initiates the telling of the narrative. A potential narrator in conversation with multiple participants first has to secure the floor. For the stories told in a group situation, this is the first step in the process. In contrast, for stories told in an interview situation, the narrator is the primary speaker and was already recognized as having the floor, so obtaining it is unnecessary. In these situations that step is omitted; instead, the narrator's first objective is to convey to the listener that a new story is about to be related.

There are different ways in which ASL signers secure the floor. Two of the techniques identified by Baker (1977) and Metzger and Bahan (2001) are utilized in the narratives I analyzed: hand waving, and connecting the new story to what was previously being discussed. Figures 5.1 and 5.2 illustrate the two techniques.

The technique used to take the floor in figure 5.1, waving one hand, is necessary because another conversation is in progress. The first two frames in figure 5.1 show that the man seated to the right of the woman attempting to get the floor is already signing. It is not until the third frame that he turns his eye gaze toward the woman and pauses to see what she will say.

In contrast, the man in figure 5.2 does not have to stop anyone else from signing in order to start his story. In this conversation the previous

Wave #1   Wave #2   Wave #3

FIGURE 5.1 *Hand-waving to secure a turn during a conversation.*

AWFUL

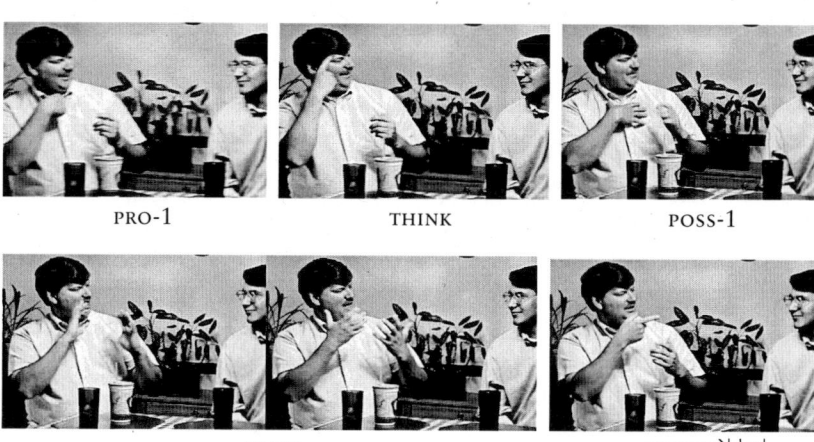

"That's terrible. It makes me think of my class."

FIGURE 5.2 *Example of securing the floor by connecting narrative to prior topic.*

signer has finished his turn and no one else has started signing. The man links his story with the previous topic by first offering his reaction to the previous speaker's story. The man signs AWFUL, "That's terrible," in the first frame of figure 5.2. This is followed by the line PRO-1 THINK POSS-1 CLASS THERE→|class|, "That makes me think of my class." The signer is stating that the topic that has just been discussed reminds him of a related experience of his own.

For stories told in situations where the narrator was already the primary storyteller, securing the floor from another signer or potential signer is not an issue. It is understood that the primary signer may sign as long as he or she wants to continue. The narrators who told stories in conversations involving a group have to secure the floor prior to the start of their narrative; therefore, the introductions to their narratives are, on average, two seconds longer than those for stories told to a single addressee.

Narrators who are already primary signers still have to set apart a new story from what came before it. They introduce new topics through overt topic marking, raising the eyebrow and tilting the head back. These topic markings are co-articulated with a lexical sign in eight of the nine

FIGURE 5.3 *Use of topicalization to introduce a new narrative.*

narratives in the first line of the introduction. Figure 5.3 shows two different narrators introducing their topics; both perform the same nonmanual topic-marking signal while signing SUBSEQUENTLY.

Each of these four signs introduces new information that suggests a new area of discussion. In addition, each of these four signs is marked as a topic by nonmanual topic marking, symbolized by ———^{t}. The context in which these signs occur helps us understand how they function to mark a new topic. The examples glossed SUBSEQUENTLY both occur immediately after the conclusion of another story. In addition, the narrative that preceded these topics transpired in time before the new ones about to be told. The precise duration of time between the events, however, is not specified. The use of the sign SUBSEQUENTLY marks a temporally ordered separation between the two events. Similarly, the lexical sign marked JUNIOR is made after the conclusion of a story about the narrator's sophomore year of college. It is not that any occurrence of the sign JUNIOR marks the beginning of a new narrative. The narrator is describing experiences from each year he was a student in college. The use of JUNIOR identifies the next time period he will describe. In addition to the signs glossed SUBSEQUENTLY, JUNIOR, and NOW in figure 5.3, ONE and #BACK occur twice as topic introductions. These signs function in a similar manner in that they distinguish the next discourse from that which preceded it. It is likely that the lexical sign and nonmanual signal work jointly to signal to the listener that a new story is about to begin. In all nine stories the narrators use T narration to identify a new story.

	rhet	
STORY	ABOUT	PRO→lmanl

"This is a story about him."

FIGURE 5.4 *Identifying the topic of a narrative.*

Once a narrator secures the floor or establishes a new topic, the focus switches to the initial telling of the story. Based on my data, it appears that this section functions as a means of providing enough information to cause the listener to want the narrator to continue. Only the most basic information is given, and none in detail. This basic information includes one to three of the following categories of information: identification of the topic, introduction of participants, identification of the location or setting of the story, and, finally, a foreshadowing of what is to come.

The introduction functions most frequently to identify the general topic of the story. This occurs in seven of the 12 introductions. Figure 5.4 and figure 5.5 illustrate the narrator introducing the topic of his or her narrative. Identifying the topic of a narrative is different from grammatically marking a topic used within a sentence that identifies what the upcoming narrative is about. Introducing narrative topics in this way is done without much detail. The examples in figure 5.4 and figure 5.5 are representative of what occurs across the narratives. The new information only serves to orient the addressee. One narrator tells a series of stories about his experience biking across the United States. He assumes that "biking cross-country" will be the ongoing topic for the listener and therefore does not repeat it for each episode in the narrative. In the introductions to stories that do not connect directly to the experience of biking, however, he does identify the topics in the introductions.

#BACK   TO   CHEER

"Returning to the topic of cheerleading."

FIGURE 5.5 *Identifying the topic of a narrative.*

Narrative Introduction / Background in ASL : 75

BEST

TEAM

FIGURE 5.6 *T narration.*

In all seven instances, the signer introduces the topic with T narration. This is signaled by eye gaze directed toward the addressee and neutral body position. Returning to figure 5.4, one notices that the narrator directs her eye gaze toward the interlocutor she previously waved at to secure the floor (figure 5.1), and in figure 5.5 the narrator directs his eye gaze toward the camera, with his body in a neutral posture.

The next most frequent function of the introduction is to identify participants in the story. This occurs in six of the 12 narratives. Notice that in figure 5.4 the topic of the story is also a participant in the story. It is therefore possible for two types of information to be conveyed in a single line. The narrator uses T narration to identify participants, although the narrator may additionally create a token or make use of a list buoy. Examples of the three types of information are reproduced in figures 5.6, 5.7, and 5.8.

The eye gaze and body position identify the signer using T narration in figures 5.6, 5.7, and 5.8. However, in figures 5.7 and 5.8 the final frames reveal the use of a token space and list buoy, respectively. The last picture in figure 5.7 is bordered in bold to indicate the creation of the token in the

HAVE   TWO   STUDENT   FROM

O-K-C-I-T-Y   THERE→|two students|

"I had two students from Oklahoma City."

FIGURE 5.7 *T narration + token.*

| PRO-1 | TELL | ONE-LIST |

"I will talk about this one friend."

FIGURE 5.8 *T narration + list buoy.*

area the index finger is pointing toward. At this point it looks as though the token can be associated either with the location Oklahoma City or with the two students. As the story continues, however, signs are directed at this space to refer to the students and not to Oklahoma City (Van Hoek, 1996). A factor that might contribute to the use of a token space is whether or not the narrator anticipates referring to the person or persons again in the upcoming story.

The third type of information conveyed in introductions is the location or setting for the story. Four of the 12 stories include location or setting in their introductions. As with participant introductions, the signer remains in the role of narrator. Within that role the narrator introduces token spaces twice. Figure 5.9 and figure 5.10 below illustrate how in one story a narrator simply states the location and in another story he introduces a token space to identify the location. The creation of token spaces happens whether or not narrators will refer to them later in the narrative. In figure 5.9 the narrator is identifying a state as the location for the next story. The state of Illinois is never referred to again after this initial identification of where the events in the story took place. In the story introduced in Figure 5.10, however, there is later reference to the firehouse. This difference in whether or not the narrator makes subsequent reference to the entity being talked about may contribute to which space or combinations of spaces are used.

| TAKE-OFF | I-L-L |

"I left there and headed to Illinois."

FIGURE 5.9 *T narration.*

| FIRE | DEPARTMENT | THERE→\|fire department\| |

"There was a firehouse."

FIGURE 5.10 *T narration + token space*.

The last function of the introduction is to give a short assessment of the upcoming story. I have labeled this function *foreshadowing*. Foreshadowing is present in three of the introductions. In two instances the narrator describes the mood of the story; two narrators use the sign FUNNY to summarize the upcoming story; and another narrator describes his story using the signs VERY EMOTIONAL. Instances of foreshadowing often provide insight into the social purpose of the story. They are an overt way in which narrators express the underlying theme of the narrative. Narrators are also able to convey this type of social information in less direct ways, which will be described in later chapters.

GENERAL CHARACTERISTICS OF THE BACKGROUND SECTION

The purpose of the background section is to give the addressee background knowledge that will be necessary to understand the main story to come. One remarkable skill narrators possess is the ability to project what these critical pieces are, which requires that the narrator assess the addressee's knowledge base and provide what might be lacking. The nature and extent of the background section is therefore dependent upon the signer's judgment about what the audience already knows. If, for example, the narrator plans to tell a story about basketball, the background section would be different if told to someone who has played for 10 years compared to someone who has never been exposed to the game. For the experienced player, a narrator may state that the opponent was playing a zone defense. The term *zone defense* triggers a knowledge schema that will be drawn on by the addressee during the telling of the story. The audience member unfamiliar with basketball would require more detailed background information, perhaps a description such as "players were required to protect a certain area on the court."

The main point of the narrator's story also influences what will be included in the background section. In the example above, if the point of the story is to describe why the opponent relied on outside shooting and therefore made a low percentage of shots, an explanation of zone defense is necessary; if the point of the story is what happened during the halftime entertainment show, it's not. An assessment of the background knowledge of the audience plus story intent helps the narrator decide what information the addressee needs to best appreciate the story.

The narrators of the stories I analyzed provide information that is both audience appropriate and topic specific. The result of this is that background sections were unique in terms of the types of information provided. While this makes analysis across narratives more complex, it also highlights the varied purposes for telling stories and the skill narrators have in constructing narratives to make them accessible to their particular listener(s).

Background sections are present in 10 of the 12 narratives. The average length of a background section is 28.1 seconds. The shortest background lasts 11 seconds and the lengthiest continues for 47 seconds. The average number of lines varies from 6 to 20, with an average length of 14.8 seconds. Extended eye closures are present at the end of eight of the 10 background sections. The average length of time the eyes remain closed is .58 seconds, ranging from .33 to .73 seconds. The eye closures are accompanied by head nods in four of the background sections. In one of the narratives told in a group setting, the eye closure is accompanied by a head turn.

FUNCTION OF BACKGROUND SECTION, PART I: SETTING AND PARTICIPANTS

A narrator's goal in both the introduction and background sections is to orient the listener. The fact that the topic, location, and participants are repeated in the background section or identified for the first time is evidence of this. In nine of the 10 background sections the narrator identifies the setting and the participants within the first two lines of the background. Figure 5.11 provides an example of this information conveyed in two lines. Figure 5.12 illustrates the information conveyed in a single line. These examples illustrate the pattern in which narrators quickly provide addressees with information to help trigger knowledge schemas for following the story to come.

| PRO→y | PAST | BOSTON | DEAF |
| CARD | PEOPLE-IN-CIRCLE | EIGHT | PLAYER |

"He played poker with eight other people at the Boston Deaf Club."

FIGURE 5.11 *Identification of setting and participants using two lines.*

This first part of the background section identifies who the participants are and what the activity is and where it is taking place. Recall that some of the introduction section already gives this information. Comparing the two sections we can see that by the end of the background section, these three pieces of information have been conveyed to the addressee, in preparation for the main story. Table 5.2 compares the information given in narrative introductions to that given in background sections. ("N/A" indicates no background section.) The numbers bolded on the right shows how many of the three types of information are provided by the end of the two sections. In all but two of the stories the background section conveys all three types of information. The story "Biking Over Water" omits identifying the topic. This story is one of a sequence of stories about the narrator's experience biking across country. It is likely that the narrator does not mention the topic again because he assumes the addressee remembers that information from the previous story. "Tobacco Story" only conveys one of the three types of information by the conclusion of the two sections. I believe this is also related to the narrator's assumption about his audience's knowledge—the story is about an experience that happened

| PRO-1 | TRY | O-U-T | GALLAUDET | CHEER |

"I tried out for the Gallaudet University cheerleading squad."

FIGURE 5.12 *Identification of setting and participants using one line.*

TABLE 5.2. *Information Provided in the Introduction and Background Sections.*

	Introduction			Background			
Story	ID Topic	ID Participants	ID Location	ID Topic	ID Participants	ID Location	Total
Conversations							
Card Game	X	X		X	X	X	3
Moment of Silence	X	X	X				3
Tobacco Story		X					1
1 on 1							
Around the World		X	X	X	X		3
Biathlon	X	X					2
Biking Over Water			X	N/A	N/A	N/A	2
Cheerleading	X			X	X	X	3
East Coast Beaches	X				X	X	3
Firehouse Fun	X		X		X		3
Flat Tires		X		X	X		3
Junior Year Football	X	X		X	X	X	2
Left Behind				X	X	X	3
Total	7	7	4	6	8	5	

a. CARD   b. CHEER

FIGURE 5.13 *Example of T narration used to identify narrative topic.*

in school, and four of the six people listening to the story attended the same school. Because of this prior knowledge, when the narrator mentions the participants by name, he apparently believes that the addressees will remember them and be able to fill in the missing context without it being overtly mentioned.

Now that we understand the type of information conveyed in this first part of the background section, it is useful to look at the types of real-space blends used to express the topic, location, and participants. In all six instances in which the topic is mentioned, the narrators use T narration. Figure 5.13 shows narrators identifying the topics "playing poker" and "trying out for the cheerleading squad." The narrator's eye gaze is directed toward her or his addressee or the camera. The body posture is neutral in both. The presence of these and the absence of blends imply that T narration is being used.

All signers use T narration when identifying the location in the background section. This information is provided in three of the narrative's background sections. The frames in Figure 5.14 are those identifying locations in "Card Game" and "Cheerleading." The eye gaze and body position are forward toward the addressees or camera, as is consistent with T narration.

The final type of information in the first part of the background sections is the identification of participants. In eight instances this information is conveyed using T narration. In three of these instances the narrators used

a. BOSTON   b. DEAF   c. GALLAUDET

FIGURE 5.14 *T narration used to identify location.*

82 : NARRATIVE INTRODUCTION/BACKGROUND IN ASL

| MAN | THERE→|man| |

"There was a man."

FIGURE 5.15 *T narration with token space.*

token spaces. Figure 5.15 shows examples of the use of a token space and a depicting space. The picture with the bolded border highlights the signer's use of the token space. The signer's eye gaze and body position in figure 5.15 tell us that the signer uses T narration throughout the two sign sequences. He points to his left side toward a token. The token is used to introduce a character and create a conceptual presence for this man in the immediate environment. This allows the narrator to refer to the man again later in the story by directing signs towards this area. The pointing of the left hand is an example of weak hand perseveration from the previous sign. (In weak hand perseveration, the signer maintains the handshape of a previous sign with the non-dominant hand while producing a new sign with the dominant hand.)

It is unclear whether or not the signer in figure 5.16 creates a real-space blend depicting a group of people sitting in a circle. One interpretation is that the signer's fingers represent multiple people, the arc movement of the two hands depicting how the players were seated around a table. In this case the signer depicts a circular arrangement of players. This utterance would be an example of T and P narration. It is also possible that the sign PEOPLE-IN-CIRCLE is not describing the particular arrangement of people, which would mean that the utterance uses only T narration.

The first part of the background section gives the addressee information about the setting and participants. In the second part, the narrator

| PEOPLE-IN-CIRCLE | EIGHT | PLAYER |

"There were eight players sitting around the table."

FIGURE 5.16 *T narration and possible P narration.*

gives the necessary background knowledge for understanding the story. This background knowledge is dependent on the particular story being told and the point that the narrator is attempting to make in telling it. For instance, in the story about the poker game, the narrator explains the rules for the specific poker game being played. This is important because comprehension of the story depends on understanding the rules of the game. In another story the narrator describes how he usually communicates with people he encounters while on his bike trip. The narrator, who is deaf, has papers prepared ahead of time that can be given to hearing people to read. On the paper it states where he began his bike journey and the location of his final destination. The narrator describes this communication system early; and it turns out to be information necessary to appreciate the story. He has apparently made the judgment that his audience would not know that this is how he routinely communicated with people on this trip.

FUNCTION OF BACKGROUND SECTION, PART II: BACKGROUND KNOWLEDGE

The second part of the background section provides the addressee with additional background knowledge needed to follow the story. A narrative is never a complete representation of what happened. Relaying every detail of an incident would be cumbersome for the narrator and tedious for the addressee. The narrative describes the event as understood by the narrator and inevitably leaves out information not known to the narrator. There is also the possibility that the narrator describes the event as he or she wishes it to be understood, which may mean intentionally omitting information that might reflect poorly on the narrator. And perhaps the narrator no longer remembers all the details of the incident. Whatever reasons contribute to the differences between what actually transpired and what is related, the background focuses the addressee's attention on the most critical pieces of information for this particular telling.

Although what qualifies as "critical information" in the narratives I studied varies from story to story, the following pattern is consistently used: The narrator, using T narration, introduces the piece of information that is of interest to the addressee. The narrator then gives specific details about this piece, relying on P narration, which uses depicting spaces, and surrogate demonstrations to fill in the detail and also to bring it into the immediate here-and-now. The signer then continues in the role of narrator and comments further about the item without the use of depicting or surrogate demonstrations. I will describe how this occurred in three of the narratives. The first example comes from the shortest background section. Next will be a narrative that requires more background information before the main story can be told. The final example is from a lengthy background section that provides a considerable amount of detailed information.

"Firehouse Fun"

This story is about an incident that happened to the narrator while on his cross-country biking trip. He biked from Virginia to Oregon over three months with a friend from college. He shares several stories about what happened along the way. In this particular narrative, the narrator and his friend have decided to spend the night in a volunteer fire department station. The building and truck are unlocked and no one is there. The story revolves around the mischief the narrator and his friend get into while spending the night there.

It is important that the addressee understand where the story takes place. The fact that it happens at a vacated fire station contributes the context for what is to come. The narrator therefore identifies and describes the location in his background. This is relatively simple information to convey, which is why I have selected it to illustrate the pattern of how general background knowledge is conveyed.

The first phase identifies the location of the event. In this story this phase starts in the introduction when the signer as the narrator identifies the location of the event as a firehouse. Figure 5.10 repeated here, illustrates how a token space is created to give a conceptual presence to the location "firehouse" in the immediate environment.

The signer continues using T narration in the second line of the background when he expands on this information (figure 5.17). The left hand pointing in the first two frames is held over from a comment the narrator made in the preceding line about the story. The determiner DET$^{\rightarrow x}$ in third frame points to the token space associated with the firehouse, created during the introduction, thereby making reference to it. It also identifies the specific firehouse being discussed in this story.

The signer continues giving a description of the firehouse. This is illustrated in figure 5.18. The narrator uses T and P narration to convey this information. The two depicting verbs in figure 5.18 show first where the

| SAY | TRUE | DET→x | VOLUNTEER | NONE |
| PEOPLE | WORK | NOTHING | | |

"It would be more accurate to call it volunteer, no one was working there, it was empty."

FIGURE 5.17 *T narration to provide additional background information.*

truck is parked and then what the building looks like. In the third frame in figure 5.18 the signer's weak hand depicts the roof of the building. His strong hand, which moves forward, depicts a truck parked in the building. The movement of the hands in the sign glossed FLAT-SURFACE-EXTEND-TO$^{\downarrow L1\text{-}L2}$ depict the shape of a large building. It is signed around the space previously occupied by the sign VEHICLE-AT$^{\downarrow L1\text{-}L2}$.

He then adds one final detail, shown in figure 5.19, before concluding the background. The narrator summarizes what he has just described using a depicting verb to show the sign on the building. NARROW-LONG-ENTITY$^{\downarrow L1\text{-}L2}$ depicts the shape of the sign on the building. In addition, the narrator makes the sign high in the space where the shape of the building was depicted. This is consistent with where a sign would be placed on the front of the firehouse and creates a more detailed depiction of the scene.

The three lines in sequence identify the information that is necessary for the addressee to understand the story. They provide a more detailed and physically immediate description of this location, and a further comment

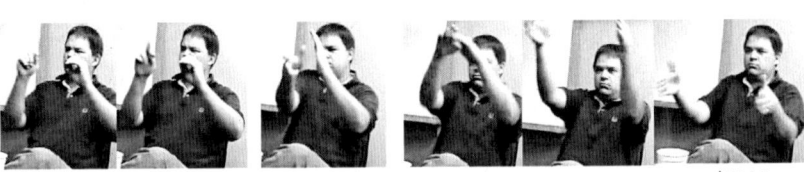

| T-R-U-C-K | S: VEHICLE-AT$^{\downarrow L1}$ | FLAT-SURFACE-EXTEND-TO$^{\downarrow L3\text{-}L4}$ |
| | W: BROAD-SURFACE$^{\downarrow L2}$ | FLAT-SURFACE-EXTEND-TO$^{\downarrow L4\text{-}L5}$ |

"A truck was parked inside a building."

FIGURE 5.18 *P narration used to describe a building.*

"The sign on the building simply said volunteer fire department."

FIGURE 5.19 *T narration used to describe a location.*

on the place. The use of depicting spaces gives the addressee information needed to construct the scene and visualize what it looked like in the space ahead of the signer. The information in this background section is relatively straightforward. In the next example, the narrator conveys more information before proceeding onto the main story. The details he provides require the use of additional types of real-space blends.

"Around the World"

"Around the World" is about another incident that happened to the narrator of "Firehouse Fun" in the state of Kansas while on his cross-country biking trip. Here he meets a man who is four states away from completing an around-the-world bicycle trip. The main story is about how the advice the man gives him improves the remainder of his bike trip to Oregon.

The narrator is deaf and normally communicates using ASL. The other man is able to hear and normally communicates using spoken English. The story revolves around the two having a conversation and a key component of the story is that the narrator is able to communicate with this man he has met for the first time. How did they communicate? The narrator recognizes the importance of resolving this issue and explains in the background how this is accomplished.

The narrator primarily uses T narration during this background; however, the simultaneous use of T and P narration does appear. He begins with an overview of how he communicated with non-ASL users on this

| PRO-1 | ALWAYS | READY | PREPARE | PAPER |

I always had a piece of paper prepared and ready.

FIGURE 5.20 *T narration being used.*

trip, then moves to a more detailed explanation of the process. He begins in figure 5.20 by stating he always has a piece of paper prepared ahead of time. Eye contact is maintained with the addressee until the final frame when the narrator looks down at the sign PAPER. He is in a neutral body position, suggesting he is using T narration.

In the next line he uses a depicting verb to demonstrate what the paper looked like. While producing the sign SQUARE-SHAPE-OBJECT$^{\downarrow L1}$ his eye gaze remains on the sign being produced. The four pictures in figure 5.21 show how he produced the sign. The narrator depicts the shape of a piece of paper in the space in front of him, giving the addressee an idea of the size and shape of the paper.

The narrator adds another layer of detail to the explanation by describing what he wrote on the paper. For this he uses a combination of T and P narration to relay what was written on the paper. The first two pictures in figure 5.22 show the narrator producing the depicting sign WRITE$^{\downarrow L1\text{-}L2}$. His eye gaze is downward and the manner in which he produces the sign depicts the writing motion. These features suggest a surrogate demonstration. After the depicting sign WRITE$^{\downarrow L1\text{-}L2}$ he signs SAY and directs his eye gaze toward the addressee. This signals the end of the surrogate demonstration. This eye contact with the addressee is maintained through the duration of the line as he states what he wrote on the paper. The narrator's use of the sign WRITE$^{\downarrow L1\text{-}L2}$ could be interpreted as P narration or P and T narration. It is unclear if the narrator is demonstrating himself writing

SQUARE-SHAPE-OBJECT$^{\downarrow L1}$

FIGURE 5.21 *Depiction of a piece of paper.*

| WRITE↓L1-L2 | SAY | WHERE | GO |

| PURPOSE | WHAT | FROM | TO |

"I wrote down on the paper where I was going,
the reason for the trip, the origination site, and the destination site."

FIGURE 5.22 *Example of T and P narration.*

something on a piece of paper, or demonstrating and describing what he is doing. The fact that his eye gaze is downward suggests that the narrator is demonstrating what he did during the past event. The remainder of the utterance is produced using T narration; his eye gaze is directed toward the addressee and he does not use any real-space blends.

In Figure 5.23 the narrator continues, clarifying what he produced. This last line is produced solely with T narration. The fact that he maintains eye contact with the addressee is consistent with T narration.

In these four lines (figures 5.20, 5.21, 5.22, and 5.23) the narrator has moved from a general concept to a detailed description of the concept and finally an explanation of how the written product will be used. To convey this information he begins with T narration in figure 5.20, uses a depicting space in figure 5.21, uses a surrogate space in the first picture of figure 5.22, and then continues with T narration without using depicting or surrogate demonstrations in figure 5.23. Recall that the goal of this second part of the background is to give the addressee background knowledge that explains how the narrator could have a conversation with someone

| CONVERSATION | QUOTE | REMAIN-THE-SAME[ITERATIVE] |

"The paper served as an entire 'conversation'
with the same information being repeated."

FIGURE 5.23 *Example of T narration.*

Narrative Introduction / Background in ASL : 89

  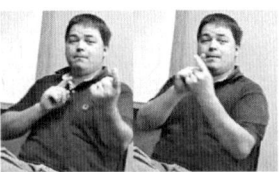

		cond/when
EACH	TIME	MEET→y.

HOLD-UP-THIN-ENTITY↓L1-L2

READ	OUR	QUOTE	CONVERSATION
	BROAD-SURFACE↓L1		

"Every time I met a new person, I would hold up one of these pieces of paper. The person could then read our 'conversation.'"

FIGURE 5.24 *Example of T and P narration.*

who communicates using spoken English. The explanation begins with these four lines, detailing the process of recording information on paper to have available for use.

The explanation continues with the narrator describing how he used these papers to communicate with people he met along the journey. We see again the pattern of moving from general topic to specific details and then a comment about the topic. In the first line of figure 5.24 the narrator explains that the use of his written paper is repeated by signing EACH TIME MEET→y[1]. When he signs MEET→y his eye gaze is directed away from the addressee as though he were looking towards the person he was meeting. He then uses P narration to describe himself holding up the piece of paper to be read. Note that this surrogate |paper| is held out in the same direction as his eye gaze while signing MEET→y. This all suggests that he created a surrogate blend with MEET→y continuing through the depiction of holding out a piece

---

1. I am unable to determine which type of nonmanual marking is being used in this example, a conditional marking or a "Wh-question" marking. The difference does not impact the analysis here.

of paper and reading it. Finally, he returns to using T narration, explaining that the person would read what was on the paper and understand where he was going. One can see that as the amount of the information increases, the number of times this pattern is used also increases.

"East Coast Beaches"

This final example is taken from the background of the narrative in which the narrator describes his first experience visiting a beach on the eastern coast of the United States. In order for the addressee to appreciate the story, the narrator has to explain in the background his experience growing up in Hawaii. This background lays the foundation for the upcoming story as it serves as a way of contrasting what happened on the East Coast beach with his expectations of what it would be like. The narrator describes how he went to the beach near his home in Hawaii daily. While at the beach he participated in activities such as snorkeling, spear fishing, and surfing. He mentions his affection for Hawaii. He establishes what his expectations were for going to the beach.

The background section for the narrative "Firehouse Fun" has a duration of 11 seconds. The background for "Around the World" is longer, with a duration of 21 seconds. The "East Coast Beaches" background section is one of the lengthiest, continuing for 37 seconds. The reason for this longer duration appears to be that the narrator attempts to build a scene about his experience growing up in Hawaii in the addressee's mind. He describes in detail the various activities he participated in while at the beaches there. He describes the frequency in which he would go to the beach. He then begins to share how much he loved his home state, mentioning in particular his love of the food. The development of this scene allows the addressee to understand the magnitude of the difference in the East Coast beach later in the story. I will not reproduce the transcript to "East Coast Beaches" here. Instead, I have included the pattern of T and P narration in the summary found in table 5.3.

T AND P NARRATION IN THE BACKGROUND SECTION

A comparison of the three stories reveals how the pattern of T narration followed by T and P narration was repeated as the narrator included more information. Table 5.3 shows the pattern of introducing a piece of information with T narration, then using P narration (depicting or surrogate

TABLE 5.3. *Pattern Used For Background Knowledge.*

Firehouse Fun	Around the World	East Coast Beaches
T narration	T narration	T narration
T narration + P narration (Depicting)	T narration + P narration (Depicting)	T narration + Buoy
T narration	T narration + P narration (Surrogate)	T narration + P narration (Surrogate)
T narration + P narration (Depicting)	T narration	T narration
	T narration + P narration (Depicting)	T narration + P narration (Surrogate)
	T narration	T narration
	T narration + P narration (Surrogate)	T narration + Token
	T narration	T narration
		T narration + P narration (Surrogate)
		T narration
		T narration + P narration (Surrogate)
		T narration
		T narration + P narration (Surrogate)
		T narration

demonstrations) to provide additional detail and bring the incident into the here-and-now in the three stories described. As the amount and complexity of detail included increases, the number of times the narrator uses the pattern also increases. The shortest background, in "Firehouse Fun," has two instances of the pattern. The pattern is used three times in the medium-length story "Around the World." In the longest background, in "East Coast Beaches," the pattern repeats six times.

The description of T narration or T and P narration used in the background sections makes it appear that there is a similar amount of P narration used as T narration. If this were the case, one could conclude that the background section focuses as much attention *on* events (function of P narration) as it does on talking *about* events (function of T narration). Returning to the examples, however, it is evident that the duration of T narration is significantly different from the duration of P narration. In figure 5.25 I have reproduced the complete background section from the

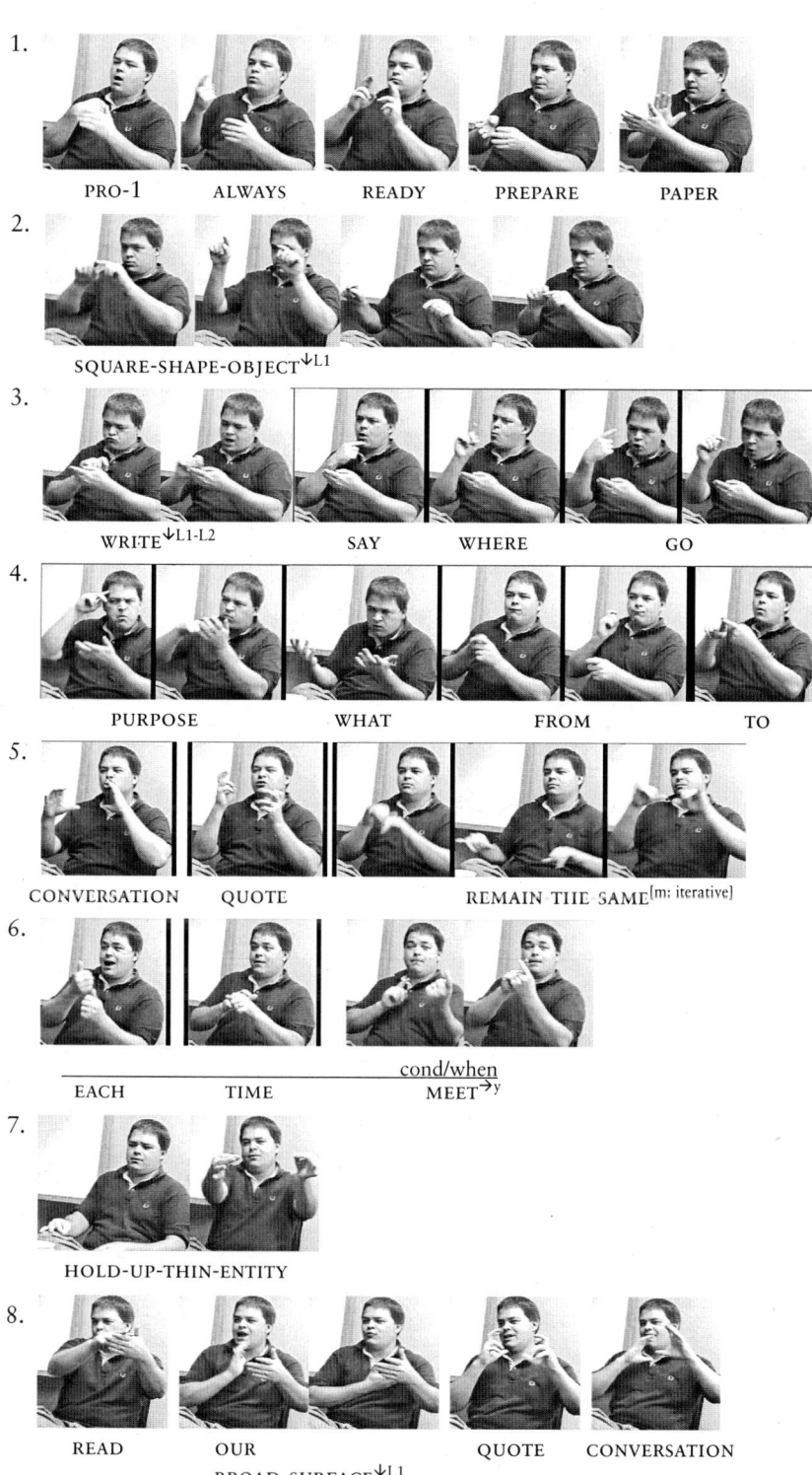

FIGURE 5.25 *Comparison of T and P narration in a background section.*

narrative "Around the World," which I previously described in detail. The background consists of eight lines, and line numbers have been added at the beginning of each new line. I have bordered in bold the pictures of all utterances that use T narration. Those that use solely P narration or P narration with T narration are not marked. There are 25 signs used; 18 (72 percent) are produced with T narration and seven (28 percent) involve P narration or simultaneous T and P narration. It is evident that T narration is the primary means of conveying information in the background section. This is consistent with the function of the background section, which is to orient the listener to the setting, participants, and other details necessary to understand the narrative. This is information *about* the events of the narrative that have not yet been described.

Chapter 6

The Structure of Main-Events Sections in ASL Narratives

Telling a narrative is a means of recapitulating personal experiences to others. As I previously argued, these narratives not only grammatically encode aspects of what took place (T narration), but, at times, they also partially recreate the past experience (P narration). T narration provides grammatically encoded information about what happened. However, P narration provides a great deal of additional information by contributing to an addressee's perceptual understanding of the story. These perceptual details elaborate the narrative events. The use of P narration is most frequent in the main-events section, in which there is a greater variety in the type of information provided than in the introduction and background sections. Table 6.1 compares the use of T and P narration in the three sections of the narratives I studied. The main-events sections include more combinations of T and P narration: there are 10 occurrences of simultaneous T and P narration, as compared to three in the introductions and nine in the background sections. The shaded columns indicate narration types that only appear in the main-events sections. Table 6.1 shows that all the introductions are made with T narration alone. The background sections use T narration alone in 70 percent of the lines, whereas in the main-events sections T narration is used in 44 percent of the lines. Narrators use simultaneous T and P narration to produce 23 percent of utterances in the background sections, compared with 48 percent in the main-events sections. P narration was used in 7 percent of the lines in both the background and main-events sections. In the 12 narratives, narrators made more use of P narration, proportionally speaking, in the main-events sections than in the introduction and background sections. The increased use of P narration in the main-events section allows the addressee to perceive additional aspects of events as they are being described by means of grammatical constructions.

Table 6.2 compares the types of information conveyed using the different narration types. The main-events section conveys 21 different types

TABLE 6.1. *Use of T or P Narration or a Combination.*

Section	T narration				T and P narration					P narration		
	T	T+Tk	T+S	T+D	N+B	T+Tk+S	T+D+S	D+S	S	Total
Introduction	18	3	0	0	0	0	0	0	0	21
Background	53	13	10	10	2	0	0	1	6	95
Main events	197	29	167	62	4	3	11	2	34	509

Note: T = T narration, Tk = token blend, S = surrogate blend, B = buoy, D = depicting blend

TABLE 6.2. *Distribution of Information Type Across Sections.*

Type of information conveyed	Introduction	Background	Main events
Physical movement - person	0	9	114
Physical movement - vehicle	0	0	8
Movement of object	0	1	5
Physical movement - animal	0	0	1
Supplemental information	3	46	166
Identification of participant	4	9	9
Identification of location	3	3	5
Identification of time	1	3	15
Constructed dialogue	0	0	2
Period of time	0	1	4
Interaction w/addressee	1	1	8
Constructed dialogue	0	3	48
Expression of emotion	0	10	54
Mental activity	0	1	12
Description of thing	0	5	12
Description of topography	0	0	12
Geographic distance	0	0	10
Arrangement of people	0	1	7
Arrangement of things	0	0	0
Mannerism	0	0	4
Listing	0	0	1
Written text	0	1	3

of information whereas the introduction only conveys five and the background 14. The main-events section conveys a greater variety of information than either the introduction or the background. The rows that are shaded indicate information that only appears in the main-events sections.

Most of the action occurs in the main-events section. This is reflected in the increased variety of types of information presented, as displayed in table 6.2. In the 12 narratives, the average length of a main-events section is 93.3 seconds; the shortest lasts 8 seconds and the lengthiest continues for 150 seconds. The number of lines varies from 8 to 112, for an average of 43.7. Extended eye closures occur at the end of nine of the 12 main-events sections. The average length of time the eyes remain closed is .5 seconds, ranging from .4 to .7 seconds (normal eye blinks last roughly .2

seconds). The eye closures are accompanied by head nods in three of the main-events sections. In two of the main-events sections the eye closures are accompanied by head turns.

BASIC FRAMEWORK OF A MAIN-EVENTS SECTION

The main-events section was defined in chapter 4 as the section in which the central events or actions are told. I define a narrative event as an event the signer describes that identifies new action or information and whose sequence reflects the order of the original events. These narrative events serve as the framework for the narrative. Elaborations of these events provide additional details and make a narrative more than a mere sequential listing of events. It takes an average of only 8.9 lines to convey the narrative events in the 12 narratives examined, ranging from 3 to 22 lines. However, an average of 34.8 lines of additional narration occur in the main-events section. These are the lines used in the elaborations. It is evident that *what* happened consumes fewer lines in the narrative than *how* or *why* something happened.

The main-events section of the narrative "Junior Year Football" helps illustrate this basic structure. In this narrative the signer describes the impact of a single loss of his football team on the team's chance to qualify for the NCAA Division III football playoffs. The main-events section describes game day. Table 6.3 provides an outline of the structure of the main-events section. The narrative events are listed in the left-hand column. The sequence of events described by the signer matches the sequence in which the actual events occurred. Additional details about the narrative event are provided by the elaborations. For example, narrative event #1 states that the game began. The elaboration describes what happened during the game: the team was outplayed. Elaborations often continue for several lines, which expand the addressee's understanding of the narrative.

In all 12 narratives, the order in which events are explained matches the order in which the actual events occurred. The number of narrative events varies depending on the length of the narrative, but there are always fewer narrative events than elaborations. The elaborations expand the events and provide additional description or details about the narrative event.

The narrator uses both T and P narration throughout the main-events section. Narrative events are described with T narration alone more often than are elaborations, which use T and P narration more frequently. Table

TABLE 6.3. *Outline of Main-Events Section Structure in "Junior Year Football."*

Narrative event	Elaboration
1. The game started.	
	We were completely overwhelmed and outplayed.
2. We lost the game 41 to 11.	
	It was so embarrassing.
3. I found out that our opponents had a challenging schedule.	
	"Now you tell us. We should have known this before."
	The captain ruined it for us.
	I shouldn't have been all "This is going to be easy."
4. Our coach was furious and bawled out the team.	
	I close my eyes to shut him out.
	His berating was intense.
	I can't even repeat what he said to you.

6.4 illustrates this pattern for the narrative "Junior Year Football." The black arrow represents the signer's production of the main-events section. The signer's use of T narration alone is represented by a bar covering the lower half of the box. When he uses both T and P narration, a bar covers the upper and lower portions of the box. There are no instances of P nar-

TABLE 6.4. *Distribution of T and P Narration in "Junior Year Football" Main-Events Section.*

ration alone in this particular main events section. Narrative events are indicated with white bars, and gray bars represent descriptions or elaborations. The narrator states the first narrative event, "the game started," using T narration. This grammatically encoded information about what happened first is then elaborated using T and P narration. The signer describes his team's performance against their opponent by saying that they were completely overwhelmed and outplayed. The use of both T and P narration provides a textual description and a visual demonstration of this reaction. Table 6.4 visually demonstrates two patterns that emerge across all the narratives. First, elaborations comprise more of the narrative than narrative events (twice as many gray bars as white bars). Second, combined T and P narration is used more often in producing elaborations than narrative events.

T narration is used to describe the narrative events in 65 percent of the lines. T narration with P narration was used in 27 percent of the lines. P narration was used alone in 5 percent of the lines. The narrative events of "Junior Year Football" help illustrate the predominant use of T narration and are illustrated in figure 6.1. The main events are captured in these four lines. In narrative events 1 through 3 the signer uses T narration. He maintains eye contact with the camera while expressing these three main events and no surrogate or depicting blends are used. In narrative event #4 the signer continues to use T narration but, in addition, conveys the intensity of the coach's reaction in the production of the signs PISS-OFF and BAWL-OUT with P narration. The signer blends with the coach and demonstrates the coach's emotion and actions.

Elaborations use T narration, P narration, and a combination of the two. Figure 6.2 illustrates a narrative event and two elaborations. The narrator first mentions that a student, Jack, was chewing tobacco. The first elaboration emphasizes that chewing tobacco is not allowed in the classroom. The second elaboration demonstrates Jack's actions. The first elaboration uses T narration and the second P narration.

There are eight narrative events in this narrative. Figure 6.2 illustrates the second of those eight events. The signer identifies the actions of one student with the articulation of J-A-C-K CHEW using T narration. The two subsequent elaborations of this narrative event accomplish two different functions. The first reinforces that tobacco chewing in class is forbidden. The signer does this by using T narration in the line IN CLASS KNOW FORBIDDEN. Evidence for T narration comes from the fact that his eye gaze is directed toward his addressees. In the second elaboration his eye

Narrative Event #1:

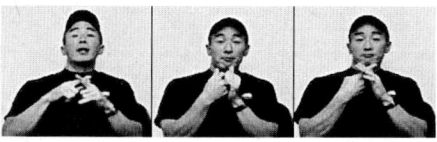

    THEN   GAME   START
"Then the game started."

Narrative Event #2:

  PRO-1   LOST   4-1

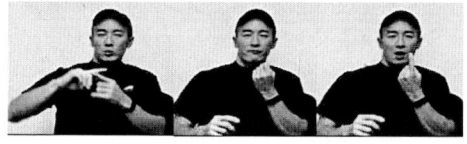

     TO   11
"We lost the game 41 to 11."

Narrative Event #3:

<u>rhet</u>
WHY   FIND   THAT   DET$^{\rightarrow x}$

    AGAINST   TOUGH

    OPPONENT   DET$^{\rightarrow x}$
"I found out that our opponents had played against tough opponents."

Narrative Event #4:

  COACH   PISS-OFF   BAWL-OUT
"Our coach was furious and bawled out the team."

FIGURE 6.1 *The four main events of "Junior Year Football."*

Narrative event:

J-A-C-K   CHEW
   "Jack started to chew."

Elaboration 1:

IN   CLASS   KNOW   FORBIDDEN
       "You know that in class it is forbidden."

Elaboration 2:

PUT-IN-MOUTH   CHEWING (continues for 1.8 seconds)
    "So he put the tobacco in his mouth and began to chew."

FIGURE 6.2 *Example of two elaborations of a narrative event.*

gaze is no longer directed toward the addressees and he moves his mouth as if he were chewing a wad of tobacco. These changes suggest that he has created a surrogate blend in which his head demonstrates the student chewing the tobacco. Since he has created a surrogate blend without lexical signs, this is P narration.

Figure 6.2 captures only the first two of nine elaborations of the narrative event J-A-C-K CHEW. The signer continues his elaboration in the subsequent seven lines adding additional details to the narrative event. Elaborations contribute details to the narrative event in all 12 of the narratives. The types of information used to elaborate the narrative events fall into the following categories: participants/setting information, movement, constructed dialogue, expressing affect, descriptions, supplemental information, and interaction with addressee. Below I describe each of these categories detailing the types of narration used to convey the information in each.

The 12 main events analyzed can be grouped into six types of stories. Three narratives are about what happened at competitive events: a biathlon, a poker game, and a football game. Two compare and contrast different situations: biking technique and geographic locations. Two describe emotional events the narrators participated in. Two describe the narrator taking part in mischievous events. One describes an obstacle that prevents the narrator from continuing his planned activity. One describes a narrator's interaction with another person. And finally, one describes a change in a situation, before and after a transformation of sorts. The topic influences the type of information that is presented and, therefore, the type of elaboration expressed between main events. For instance, the story that focuses on the narrator's interaction with another person has 14 instances of constructed dialogue, whereas the story that compared and contrasted different situations only had two instances of constructed dialogue. In spite of this variation, the narratives share the characteristic of having a few main events and many elaborations to give life to them.

ELABORATION OF NARRATIVE EVENTS

This section describes the six ways in which the narrators expanded the narrative events. This information fleshes out, often in vivid detail, the particulars of a scene or action. The categories I describe are those that emerged from the narratives I analyzed. There are undoubtedly additional types of information that a narrator can include that are not mentioned here because the narrators do not produce them in these 12 narratives. The categories that did occur, however, occurred frequently. Later, I will discuss a seventh category, which I have labeled "interaction with addressee."

Participants/Setting

The participants/setting category includes ways in which narrators elaborate who the participants are in the story, where the story takes place, and when the event happened. This category contributes additional information that may not have been included in the previous background section, or it repeats information from that section. In narratives without a background section, the elaborations that occur between narrative events may include the initial presentation of information about participants or settings. T narration is used for all three types of the information conveyed.

L-I-S-A
POINTER→x

FIGURE 6.3 *Example of narrator creating a token blend.*

Identification of story participants occurs four times in the 12 narratives analyzed. In three of the four instances the narrator spells the characters' names. Two times the narrator also provides a name sign for the character whose name has just been spelled. In the fourth example the signer produces the lexical sign MAN without further elaboration.

Narrators often create token blends when identifying a participant. Figure 6.3 illustrates an example of this. The signer identifies a character named Lisa in his story by spelling her name. His eye gaze is toward the camera indicating he is using T narration. While he spells the character's name with his right hand, he points to an area to his left with his left hand. The area to the left that the POINTER buoy is directed toward is now blended with Lisa, resulting in the token |Lisa|. Later in the story the narrator directs signs to |Lisa| when he wants to talk about Lisa.

Similarly, in the identification of a location, a narrator mentions the name of a specific place, like the name of a state, or even a more generic description such as "outdoors." Figure 6.4 illustrates two such examples. The signer in figure 6.4a identifies the destination for his cross-country bicycle trip. The signer in figure 6.4b identifies where a competition was held.

a. O-R-E-G-O-N

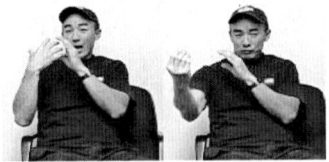

b. OUTSIDE

FIGURE 6.4 *Signs used to identify the location in a narrative.*

"It was Labor Day weekend during my freshman year."

FIGURE 6.5 *Narrator identifying time an event occurred.*

The most common way to identify time is to use signs identifying time of day, such as MORNING or NIGHT, which are used in over half the instances (58 percent). Narrators also identify time according to what time of year the event happened, as in figure 6.5. The signer in figure 6.5 identifies the time of year when he signs L-A-B-O-R WEEKEND.

Narrators also identify how long an event continued. Six of the nine times the duration of time is identified with the sign ALL-DAY.

Movement

A second method for elaborating narrative events is to describe movement. I have divided movement into two categories. Locomotion is movement that involves an entity moving from one location to another. Non-locomotion is movement in which a part of an entity moves. The movement of people includes examples of both locomotion and non-locomotion. The movement of vehicles and objects is described in terms of locomotion.

There are 128 instances in which movement is described in an elaboration. Of the 128, 114 involve the movement of a person. The movement of vehicles is described in eight instances, the movement of an object in five, and there is one description of the movement made by an animal.

DESCRIPTION OF NON-LOCOMOTION

The physical movement of a person is the most frequent type of motion described in the 12 narratives. Narrators frequently describe the movement of body parts, including arm/hand, legs/feet, and head/eyes, rather than the movement of the entire person from one place to another. There is one instance in which movement of the whole body is described. Both T and P narration are used in 77 percent of the lines in which the movement of a body part is described.

The movement of a character's arm or hand is demonstrated 37 times. This makes it the most frequently demonstrated body part. In most cases the signer conveys two pieces of information simultaneously: the motion of the arm, from shoulder to wrist, and what the hand was used for. Figure 6.6 illustrates two examples of this. In figure 6.6a the narrator demonstrates the character in the story handing a piece of paper to another person. Eye contact is no longer toward the addressee, indicating that the signer has created a surrogate demonstration. The verb HAND-THIN-ENTITY-TO$^{\rightarrow y}$ encodes the meaning "hand thin entity to someone." This verb simultaneously depicts the motion of handing an entity to someone. The signer moves his hand to the area that is associated with another surrogate character, which indicates his own surrogate character's interaction with that character. The use of the surrogate blend allows the narrator to represent the action of the character's arm. The movement from his side, upwards and to his left and back down resembles the motion of handing an object to another person. The handshape of his right hand suggests he could be holding a piece of paper. This combined use of T narration ("hand thin entity to") and P narration (demonstrating the movement of the hand in moving the object) allows for simultaneous expression of lexical information and demonstration of the movement.

The narrator in figure 6.6b is at the point in her narrative at which one person punched another. She encodes this action with the verb PUNCH$^{\rightarrow y}$.

a. HAND-THIN-ENTITY-TO$^{\rightarrow y}$

b. PUNCH$^{\rightarrow y}$

FIGURE 6.6 *Example of arm/hand movement.*

Her face, body, and arm blend with the person punching in this surrogate blend. Her eye gaze is no longer toward the addressee and her intense facial expression is similar to that of an angry person. These characteristics provide evidence of the surrogate blend. The motion of the arm depicts a punching motion, but it does not replicate one. Notice that the fist does not start near the shoulder with the elbow completely bent and it does not finish in this position either. She does add a slight backwards jerk that makes it appear as if she made contact with another surface. The result is a partial demonstration of what happened. As in figure 6.6a, the narrator combines the motion of the arm with the configuration of the hand to create the intended demonstration.

There are also surrogate blends in which the movement of the arm is in focus but the hand position is not significant. Figure 6.7 illustrates one of the two examples of this. The narrator is describing the actions of the race starter of a biathlon. The narrator's face and arms blend with the starter as he drops his hand in much the same way a race starter does to signal to competitors to start running. Figure 6.7 illustrates the starter's behavior with the change in eye gaze and arm position of the |starter|. Again, the action of dropping the arm does not replicate the actual motion used but partially demonstrates it. In this instance, the handshape does not contribute additional meaning. The motion being demonstrated is the downward movement of the arm.

The next physical motions highlighted by T and P narration are activities involving the movement of the legs and feet. There are 19 examples in the narratives analyzed. Because all the narrators were recorded in a seated position, their ability to use their legs for surrogate demonstrations was limited. Narrators move their legs when possible, but they also rely upon other movements linked to the movement of the legs.

In the narrative about competing in a biathlon, the narrator describes the biking leg of the race. Blended surrogate spaces are used to demonstrate the action of the biathlete. The |biathlete| in the blended space is furiously biking. One instance is illustrated in figure 6.8. The signer's legs

RAPIDLY LOWERS ARM

FIGURE 6.7 *Example of arm movement, hand not involved.*

PEDAL-BIKE

FIGURE 6.8. *Example of leg movement during the sign* PEDAL-BIKE.

and face are blended with the conceptualized biathlete. The signer lifts his legs up and down to represent the pedaling motion. If a person were actually on a bike pedaling, the feet would be moving in circular motion. The fact that the signer is seated in a chair rather than mounted on a bike makes duplicating that motion difficult. He is able to move his legs up and down such that the knees are lifted and lowered. The addressee relies on knowledge about bicycling to create the image of a person pedaling a bike. The facial expression conveys the intense effort that accompanies the pedaling. The verb PEDAL-BIKE identifies the particular action the signer is demonstrating. Because the movement of the legs only partially demonstrates the action, it is unlikely an addressee would be able to comprehend the meaning without the simultaneous T narration.

The motion of a character's head, eyes, and mouth is demonstrated 14 times. T and P narration are used in seven of the eight instances in which a narrator describes movement of gaze. Figure 6.9 reproduces an example from chapter 2 to illustrate an example of this type of motion. The narrator describes the school principal looking at students in an attempt to figure out who has been spitting tobacco out of the classroom window. The signer creates a surrogate blend in which his face and eye gaze blend with the face and eye gaze of the principal; the verb in figure 6.9 describes the movement of the |principal|'s eye gaze. Again, simultaneous T and P narration convey this information. Without the articulation of the sign

LOOK-AROUND^∪ↄ

FIGURE 6.9. *Description of eye-gaze movement.*

a. Spitting

b. Open and close mouth

FIGURE 6.10 *Demonstrations of mouth movements.*

LOOK-AROUND$^{\cup\supset}$ an addressee may not understand the significance of the signer rotating his head from left to right. Likewise, without seeing the facial expression and direction of the eye gaze the addressee would not understand that the narrator was demonstrating what happened in the classroom.

When the movement of the mouth is being described, signers use P narration alone. The examples in figures 6.10a and b illustrate two types of mouth movements. The narrator in figure 6.10a is describing a student spitting chewing tobacco. In figure 6.10b he is describing how a student opened his mouth to show he was not chewing tobacco. The signer creates a surrogate blend in which his face and body blend with the face and body of the student. This allows the addressee to directly observe the action of the |student|. The signer's body moves forward in his chair as he demonstrates the |student| spitting. The mouth movements, though they are difficult to perceive in figure 6.10a, involve pursing the lips and then releasing them. In figure 6.10b the signer demonstrates the |student| opening and closing his mouth. T narration is not used in either of these utterances. The surrogate blend itself clearly expresses what happened.

Finally, narrators use surrogate blends to describe the movement of the entire body.

There are eight instances of this type in the narratives analyzed. Because they are seated, the signers are never in exactly the same position as the movement being demonstrated. The signers modify the movements, however, to accommodate their seated positions. Figure 6.11, from the narrative about a biathlon, gives one example of how a signer conveys

Changing clothes

FIGURE 6.11 *Demonstration of action that involves the entire body.*

movements that involve the entire body. The signer is explaining what happened at the transition area between the running and the cycling leg of the competition. A competitor normally changes shorts and shoes and puts on a helmet and gloves during a transition. To accomplish these tasks, one must move the entire body. The signer creates a surrogate blend in which his entire body blends with that of the biathlete. The |biathlete| leans forward and brings his right knee up, presumably to reach his shoe. At the same time he moves his arms and hands as if he is grabbing and throwing his clothes on the ground. The surrogate blend in figure 6.11 does not match exactly how one would take off a pair of shoes and put another on or change one's shorts; however, within the context of the story, it is clear what is being demonstrated.

DESCRIPTION OF LOCOMOTION

A second type of motion involves entities moving from one location to another. Signers most commonly described this type of movement using depicting blends, which occurred in 83 percent of the descriptions of locomotion. Depicting verbs symbolically express and visually depict what happened; they also allow the signer to depict the path and manner of the movement.

The narrator in figure 6.12 is explaining how he ran down the sloped beach until he reached the ocean. The use of partitioning allows the signer to project parts of himself into the blend. The signer's movement down

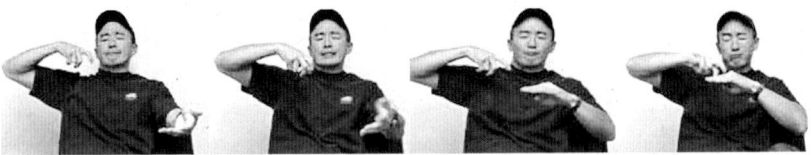

BIPED-MOVE-TO↓L1-L2
BROAD-SURFACE↓L2

FIGURE 6.12 *Depicting verb used to describe locomotion of a person.*

the sloped beach is mapped onto the depicting verb BIPED-MOVE-TO^{↓L1-L2} produced by his right hand. The ocean maps onto his left hand, which produces BROAD-SURFACE^{↓L1}. His facial expression signals that a surrogate blend has been created and demonstrates the effort used while moving. In the first four pictures the |swimmer| is moving on sand and the signer's facial expression suggests moving with little effort. Once the verb BIPED-MOVE-TO^{↓L1-L2} makes contact with BROAD-SURFACE^{↓L2} in the fourth picture the |swimmer| has reached the |water|. The signer's facial expression changes to reflect the increased effort required to move through water. The verb BIPED-MOVE-TO^{↓L1-L2} begins near the signer's right shoulder and his hand moves downward and forward. This path traveled by the hand and the path in the past event space blend to create the |travel path|. This provides a partial visual depiction of the person moving down the slope of a beach to the water.

The locomotion of vehicles also appears in the narratives. There are nine instances of the narrator describing the movement of vehicles, specifically, bicycles and boats. All descriptions of bicycle movement are made with the use of depicting blends. As with the depicting demonstrations used to describe the movement of a person, the focus is on the path and manner of the movement of the bicycle. Figure 6.13 provides an example of a depicting verb being used to describe vehicle movement.

The narrator in figure 6.13 describes how he avoids damaging his tires while biking by carefully maneuvering around any potentially dangerous objects such as rocks, nails, or glass. The 3 handshape is the lexically specified handshape in the verb VEHICLE-WIND-ALONG^{↓L1-L2}. Although difficult to see in the still pictures, the signer moves his right hand, which represents his bike, side to side in the production of the depicting verb. This motion depicts the side-to-side movement used to navigate around the obstacles. Simultaneously, his hand moves away from his body, depicting the bicycle's forward motion. The signer's facial expression contributes information to

VEHICLE-WIND-ALONG^{↓L1-L2}
BROAD-SURFACE^{↓L1}

FIGURE 6.13 *Depicting verb used to describe locomotion of a vehicle.*

the description as well: his lips are lightly pressed together in a nonmanual marker that suggests doing something carefully. This depicting demonstration then provides information about the path and manner of the bike's movement between two locations.

When describing vehicles narrators generally focus on the path and manner of the movement. Depicting demonstrations lend themselves to expressing this type of information, which is likely why all examples of vehicle movement involve depicting demonstrations. Narrators' facial expressions also contribute valuable information indicating how to interpret the manner of the movement.

The remaining two categories of movement described in the main-events sections involve the movements of objects and animals. In the 12 narratives there are five descriptions of objects moving and a single example of the motion of an animal. This single example of animal motion does not allow me to make any generalizations here. I will therefore only describe the motion of objects.

In all descriptions of objects moving, narrators use depicting blends to describe the motion. The narrator in figure 6.14 describes how the principal storms into the classroom unannounced. The door is mapped onto the signer's right hand. The motion used in the depicting verb depicts the motion of the actual object. The fingers on the hand that represents |door| are pressed together. Doors typically have solid surfaces, and the verb selected has a handshape that represents this characteristic. The extending of the signer's wrist depicts the motion of an object rotating on a hinge.

In other instances the path of the object's movement is shown in relation to another entity. An example of this is shown in figure 6.15. The narrator describes how a wad of tobacco was spit through a window that was slightly open. The signer's right hand blends with the opening of the window. It creates the space that the other hand depicting the path of the wad of tobacco will pass through and becomes a depicting buoy that

DOOR-SWING-OPEN^{↓L1-L2}

FIGURE 6.14 *Depicting verb describing movement of an object.*

OBJECT-PASS-THROUGH↓L1-L2
(depicting buoy)

FIGURE 6.15 *Depicting verb describing movement of an entity in relation to another entity.*

continues to be used by the signer. The left hand demonstrates the path along which the wad traveled.

Elaborations such as these that provide details about how people, vehicles, or objects move are the second most common type of elaboration in the narratives analyzed. As shown above, these descriptions can involve either locomotion or non-locomotion. Although signers most often use T and P narration simultaneously to describe non-locomotion and locomotion, the type of blends they use differs. Surrogate blends are more often used to describe non-locomotion, and depicting blends are used to describe locomotion. Table 6.5 summarizes the distribution of narration type and blend type in the narratives. T narration alone is used to describe locomotion and non-locomotion of people, vehicles, and objects. P narration alone is used in the description of non-locomotion of people. Simultaneous T and P narration is used to describe both locomotion and non-locomotion

TABLE 6.5. *Distribution of Narration Types Used to Describe Movement.*

	Movement			
	Non-locomotion	Locomotion		
Narration Type & Blend Type	Person	Person	Vehicle	Object
T Narration	X	X	X	X
P narration – Surrogate Blends	X			
T Narration + P narration – Surrogate Blends	X	X		
T Narration + P narration – Depicting Blend	X 0	X	X	X

Narrative Main Events in ASL

of people, vehicles, and objects. Surrogate blends, however, are used to demonstrate only the movement of people.

These patterns fit with the findings of other researchers that sign-language users find it more efficient and effective to demonstrate a movement rather than describe it using lexical signs, a tendency that Engberg-Pedersen (1999) calls a "signed-language narrative ideal." The fact that T narration is present in signed narratives, however, is consistent with the findings of Taub and Galvan (2001), who suggest that events are separated into different pieces and presented sequentially. A signer may use both T and P narration to accommodate the need to separate the event into parts, relying on T narration to identify an aspect and P narration to then demonstrate the motion.

Constructed Dialogue

Constructed dialogue between characters is a third way that narrators elaborate on narrative events. Nine of the 12 narratives contained constructed dialogue with 48 instances distributed across these nine. As explained in chapter 1, constructed dialogue is dialogue presented as if it is the actual utterance was produced during the past event, even though it is primarily the creation of the narrator (Tannen 1989). Narrators use constructed dialogue to convey the utterance of a single person or present the interaction between people.

A direct quote is a type of constructed dialogue that is uttered as if the speaker or signer produced it. The following example shows how constructed dialogue can be presented in English.

Jamie said, "This is an interesting book."

The words within the quotes are supposed to represent the words the speaker actually uttered. A direct quote in spoken English can be preceded by a clause that introduces the quote. In the example above the clause *Jamie said* identifies who uttered the words and functions to mark the beginning of the constructed dialogue. Constructed dialogue can be produced without an introducer. An English speaker often utters dialogue with a different tone of voice or intonation. This different voice quality signals to the addressee that the utterance is that of another person. An example I presented in chapter 1 is repeated here in figure 6.16. The raised pitch of the narrator signals that the utterance "Hey, where did you go?" is to be attributed to a character in the narrative.

> Narrator: So she looks around . . .
> Hey, where did you go? [spoken with a raised pitch]
> Addressee: [Laughs.]

FIGURE 6.16 *Direct quote without an introducer.*

In the 12 narratives I found examples of direct quotes uttered with and without the use of introducers. I will begin with an example of constructed dialogue that does use an introducer. The narrator in figure 6.17 is telling a story about playing football while he was in college. He describes one loss that resulted in his team not being selected to participate in the NCAA Division III playoffs. He explains that the reason they lost was because they underestimated their opponent. The narrator produces constructed dialogue of what the team captain told the players before the game began.

The narrator introduces the constructed dialogue with the topic CAPTAIN DET$^{\rightarrow x}$, produced with T narration. Evidence of this includes the eye gaze directed at the addressee and the lack of surrogate or depicting blends. The token |captain| is located in the space to his right. The narrator directs DET$^{\rightarrow x}$ toward |captain|, thereby making reference to the captain. The immediately following constructed dialogue represents what the captain signed. The signer creates a surrogate blend in which his face and arms are blended with the captain in the event space. He then signs PRO$^{\rightarrow |opponent|}$ NOTHING, his eye gaze is directed to his left as if talking to his teammates. There is no one in real space to his left, but he is facing |players| in that direction in a surrogate space. The signs as articulated fill

CAPTAIN   DET$^{\rightarrow x}$ PRO$^{\rightarrow |opponent|}$ NOTHING

The captain said, "That team is nothing."

FIGURE 6.17 *Constructed dialogue with an introducer.*

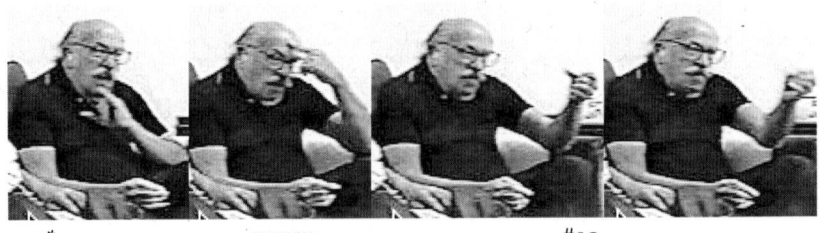

a. I* THINK #SO
Principal: "I thought so!"

                                          wh
b. HOW   KNOW   PRO→|principal|

*The gloss "I" is used rather than PRO-1 to reflect the use of the S.E.E. sign invented to represent the English pronoun "I."

FIGURE 6.18 *Constructed dialogue between characters.*

a large area in the signing space. This difference in the production of the signs is additional evidence that he is signing as |captain|.

Fourteen of the instances of constructed dialogue involve conversations between characters. These exchanges demonstrate the integration between T and P narration. The narrator in figure 6.18 describes how, despite a student's earlier success at hiding the evidence of his misbehavior, the principal discovered proof that he was chewing tobacco. Two surrogate blends are used in this exchange. The constructed dialogue of the |principal| is represented in figure 6.18. The signer's face and left hand blend with that of the principal in the event space. The signer directs his eye gaze toward an imagined group ahead of him and produces I THINK #SO. The dialogue represents what the |principal| signed in the event space.

The new surrogate blend is signaled with the signer's change in eye gaze, pictured in figure 6.18b. The signer's face and left arm blend with that of himself as a student responding to the principal.[1] His eye gaze is directed up toward the imagined |principal|. The lexical signs produced

---

1. It is possible that this is an example of a category of constructed dialogue Tannen labels *choral dialogue*. This interpretation would mean the signing represents all the students in the classroom. However, the signer clarifies in the two lines immediately following this utterance that the speaker was a single student.

in this blend are not T narration. The signer effectively uses P narration to represent the character's T narration during the classroom event; the addressee has to construct the meaning from other input such as the narrator's eye gaze, his facial expressions, and where his signs are directed in the signing space.

This example also illustrates how a narrator can include additional social information into the narrative with the choice of signs used in the constructed dialogue. The story is about deaf students' experience at a school. At the time the narrator was a student most of the faculty was hearing and probably did not use ASL. The narrator's use of the initialized sign "I" in figure 6.18 is a way in which the narrator signals this social aspect of the experience to the addressees. The production of constructed dialogue with this lexical sign conveys this additional social dimension to the addressees.

Indirect speech is a representation of dialogue that is not uttered in the way the person produced it. A narrator could use direct speech such as, "Jamie said, 'I play hockey every Sunday.'" The narrator could present the same dialogue using indirect speech, for example, "Jamie said he plays hockey every Sunday." The different prosodic cues signal the use of indirect speech. To identify the use of indirect speech in ASL one needs to rely on the presence or absence of P narration. More specifically, constructed dialogue always makes use of surrogate blends. Indirect quotes are always signed using T narration.

Figure 6.19 illustrates an example of indirect speech. The narrative is about how the signer met an experienced bicyclist during his cross-country bicycle trip. This cyclist gave him advice on how to be a more efficient bike traveler. The narrator uses the rhetorical question SAY WHAT to introduce the indirect speech and then produces PRO-1 BETTER HABIT, which characterizes what the experienced bicyclist said. The signer signs PRO-1 twice, which suggests changing his habits was something the inexperienced bicyclist should do. The narrator's eye gaze is directed at the addressee and he does not use P narration. There were only nine instances of indirect speech in the 12 narratives compared with 34 instances of direct speech.

To distinguish between T and P narration, it is necessary to understand the difference between constructed dialogue and indirect speech in ASL narratives. P narration is always used when a narrator uses constructed dialogue, although this dialogue may be introduced first with T narration. Indirect speech is always produced with T narration.

	rhet
SAY	WHAT

"What did he say to me?"

PRO-1   BETTER   HABIT

"He told me I needed better habits."

FIGURE 6.19 *Indirect quote.*

Expressing Affect

A fourth type of elaboration involves narrators demonstrating an emotional response to an event. This occurs 54 times in the 12 narratives. Sixty-five percent of the instances use a combination of T and P narration or P narration alone to express the emotion. T narration alone is used in the other 19 instances (35 percent).

The most common way for a signer to express a reaction (29 instances) is with the use of T and P narration. The signers use their ability to partition the body to allow for different information to be simultaneously produced. The signer in figure 6.20 is describing his reaction to losing a football game to a weaker team. The signer blends his facial expression

|football player|

EMBARRASS

"I was so embarrassed."

FIGURE 6.20 *Expression of emotion with T and P narration.*

with that of himself as a football player in the event space. His hands are those of the signer in real space, which articulate the sign EMBARRASS. This lexical sign describes the reaction. The facial expression contributes additional meaning, suggesting perhaps anguish or disbelief. This layering of information through partitionable body parts creates a rich depiction of emotion. Both the input of the facial expression and the lexical sign contribute to the addressee's comprehension of how the signer felt at that moment in the story.

Although less frequent, P narration alone appears six times in the 12 narratives. Two examples are provided in figure 6.21. The signer's face in figure 6.21a has blended with his face as a student in the event space. The principal has just revealed that tobacco spit is covering the flagpole outside their classroom, and the |student| reacts with surprise to the principal's evidence. The signer's face in figure 6.21b has blended with the face of a poker player in the event space. The poker player reacts to losing a large bet and the signer depicts the angry reaction of the |poker player|. These facial expressions are maintained longer than those accompanying signs in other parts of the narrative. In figure 6.21a the signer holds his expression for 1.16 seconds; the signer in figure 6.21b holds her expression for .62 seconds.

Ekman and Friesen (1975) suggest that there are six "basic" expressions of emotions that appear to be universal among humans: anger, disgust, fear, happiness, sadness, and surprise. Ekman argues that people use distinctive universal signals to express these emotions; when shown these expressions people of all languages correctly identify the associated emotion. The two expressions illustrated in figure 6.21, surprise and anger, are two of these basic six. The fact that they are produced with P narration alone may be because the meaning is transparent to the addressee. The narrators use these expressions to demonstrate their reactions during the event. The narrator in figure 6.21a is not surprised at the moment of telling the narrative, but he selects this basic expression to demonstrate his past reaction. In

a. suprise   b. anger

FIGURE 6.21 *Expressing emotion with P narration.*

ENJOY B-E-A-C-H
"I enjoy the beach."

FIGURE 6.22 *Expression emotion with T narration.*

contrast, the facial expression illustrated in figure 6.20 is accompanied by the sign EMBARRASS. In this example the simultaneous production of the facial expression and lexical sign provide descriptions of the signer's reaction, because "embarrassed" is not a basic expression of emotion.

T narration is also used to describe emotions. These purely grammatical descriptions occur 17 times in the narratives analyzed. When T narration is used, the narrator describes what a character was feeling rather than demonstrates an emotional response for the addressee. Figure 6.22 illustrates emotion being conveyed with T narration. The signer is originally from Hawaii and is telling about his first experience visiting a beach on the East Coast of the United States. He describes the many differences between the beaches and ocean in Hawaii and the one he visited. He describes his reaction to this experience. The signer's eye gaze is directed toward the addressee and no blends are used to express the information. The signer is smiling while producing the signs ENJOY B-E-A-C-H. This positive comment is complimented by the facial expression, which reflects his happiness during the past event.

When expressing reactions of emotion in a narrative, the signers in the 12 narratives most often made use of a combination of T and P narration. The examples presented demonstrate the range of emotions that can be described. Signers do not simply label the emotions but demonstrate them as well. The facial expressions and body positions contribute additional meaning to the lexical signs produced and enhance an addressee's comprehension of the emotion.

Descriptions

A fifth type of elaboration found in the narratives analyzed is descriptions of objects, topography, and arrangements of people. Depicting verbs are used in 74 percent of these descriptions. The use of depicting verbs enables a narrator to describe the shape of an object, as well as how it

CYLINDRICAL-ENTITY-EXTEND-TO^{↓L1-L2}

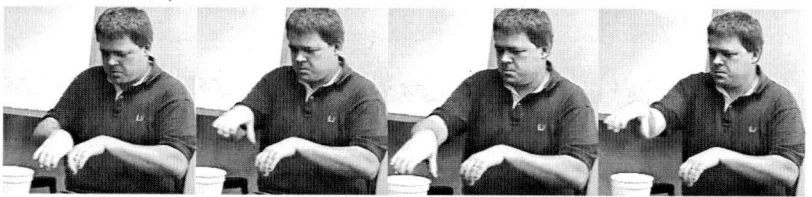

CYLINDRICAL-ENTITY-BE-AT^{↓L1} CYLINDRICAL-ENTITY-BE-AT^{↓L1} CYLINDRICAL-ENTITY-BE-AT^{↓L1} CYLINDRICAL-ENTITY^{↓L1} BUOY

FIGURE 6.23 *Depicting verbs used to describe an object.*

was configured in space. The narrator in figure 6.23 describes a type of gate called a cattle guard, used by farmers to prevent cows from walking off their property. Different than a gate that swings open and closed, a cattle guard uses evenly spaced short poles placed over a shallow ditch spanning the entrance to the property; the cattle are unable to balance on the poles and therefore cannot cross the opening. The signer first describes the poles using the depicting verb CYLINDRICAL-ENTITY-EXTEND-TO^{→L1-L2}. The handshapes demonstrate the cylindrical shape of the poles. The narrator separates his hands, thereby depicting length. He then moves his right hand next to his left, then lifts it and moves it forward, lowers his hand, then again lifts it, moves its forward, and lowers it. This repeated movement depicts several poles placed near each other.

The use of depicting verbs also allows signers to demonstrate where entities are in relation to other entities and are used by narrators to describe how people were arranged. For example, the narrator in figure 6.24 describes how he and his friends were seated in their classroom. The narrator identifies three people when he signs SANDY PRO-1 J-A-C-K. His body moves with the articulation of each person. His body moves to his right as he signs SANDY, it is at a neutral position as he signs PRO-1, and he leans slightly to his left when he produces J-A-C-K. He then uses the depicting verb TWO-SIT-BESIDE-1^{↓L1} to demonstrate how they were seated. The signer's body blends with his body in the event space; his left and right hand represent Sandy and Jack in the event space. When he articulates TWO-PEOPLE-SIT-NEXT-TO^{↓L1} it represents |Sandy|, |Signer|, and |Jack| seated in a row.

Narrative Main Events in ASL : 121

| SANDY | PRO-1 | J-A-C-K | TWO-SIT-BESIDE-1^{↓L1} |

"Sandy, Jack, and I sat next to one another."

FIGURE 6.24 *Depicting verb used to describe the arrangement of people.* (Note that SANDY is a name sign.)

Narrators also describe a person in relation to other entities. The narrator in the next example describes the unusual places he slept during his cross-country bicycle trip. In this example he spent the night in a vacant firehouse and slept in the cab of the fire truck. His description of this arrangement is illustrated in figure 6.25. The signer produces STEERING-WHEEL, which an addressee understands is located in the cab of the truck. His left hand remains as a depicting buoy of the steering wheel while his right hand produces the sign BIPED-LAY-DOWN^{↓L1}. This depicting verb demonstrates how a person might lay down. The spatial arrangement between the |steering wheel|, the location of which can be deduced from the location of the depicting buoy, and BIPED-LAY-DOWN^{↓L1}, describes where the |person| laid down in relation to the |steering wheel|. The fact that the size of the person and steering wheel do not represent real-world proportions does not impact the addressee's comprehension.

There are six instances (14 percent) of descriptions in which only T narration is used. The narrator in figure 6.26, for example, is describing the coarseness of sand at the beach he visited. The narrator uses the grammatical expression VERY THIN to describe the sand. The signer squints his eyes throughout the articulation of the sign. This nonmanual sign associated with thinness accompanies the lexical description.

 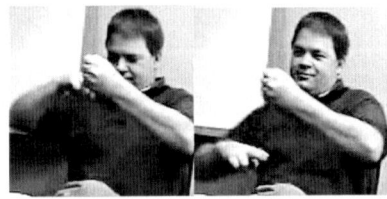

STEERING-WHEEL   BIPED-LAY-DOWN^{↓L1}
                              DEPICTING BUOY

FIGURE 6.25 *Depicting verb describing arrangement of person in relation to another entity.*

| S-A-N-D | VERY | THIN |

The sand was very thin.

FIGURE 6.26 *Description of an entity with T narration.*

Supplemental Information

A sixth type of expansion is one I call supplemental information. These elaborations provide additional information an addressee may need to know in order to comprehend or appreciate the story. The narrator provides these details as the narrative is told, highlighting a point or offering insight into what the narrator was thinking at that moment in the story.

There are 50 instances of supplemental information in the narratives analyzed. Forty of these lines are produced with T narration (80 percent). The other 10 lines are produced with a combination of T narration and P narration.

The three lines in figure 6.27 show an example of a supplemental elaboration that makes the reason for a narrative event more explicit. In the narrative event, the narrator states that he is running the race alone. He elaborates by describing his reason for this decision. The signer directs his eye gaze toward the addressee throughout the three lines. He does not create any blends, although he does make use of the previously existing token |Lisa| by directing DET$^{\rightarrow |Lisa|}$ toward that token.

In other instances the narrator provides insight into what another character was thinking. For example, in figure 6.28 the narrator tells her addressees what one poker player assumes his opponent's cards are. As with the previous example, the signer uses T narration in this explanation. Her eye gaze is toward her addressees and she does not create any blends.

Supplemental information, then, is a means for the narrator to elaborate a narrative event. It provides information the addressee would not otherwise have access to, or information an addressee chooses to emphasize for some reason. Narrators may explicitly state a motivation for a narrative event, or they may describe how other characters interpreted a narrative event. When supplemental information is provided in elaborations, T narration is most often used.

PRO-1 DON'T-WANT WITH DET→|Lisa|
"I didn't want to run with her."

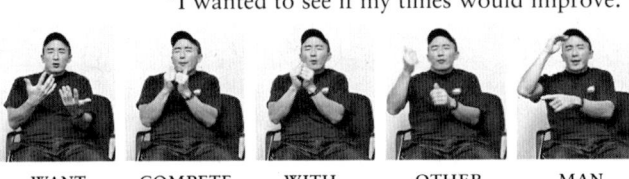

PRO-1   WANT   SEE   TIME   #IF   HAVE   IMPROVE
"I wanted to see if my times would improve."

WANT   COMPETE   WITH   OTHER   MAN
"I wanted to compete with other men
(to make improvement more likely)."

FIGURE 6.27 *Example of an elaboration providing supplemental information.*

Interactions with Addressee

The seventh category, managing interactions with an addressee, does not expand on the main events, but rather creates interactions between the narrator and the addressee. In all 12 narratives the narrator initiates these interactions. The narrator asks the addressee(s), for example, whether or not they understand what is being described. If the response from the addressee(s) is negative, the narrator provides further elaboration.

THINK   DET→|player 1| NEXT   WILD
"He thought that the next card would be a wild card."

ADD   MAKE   5   QUEEN
"The addition of that card to Harvey's hand would give him five queens."

FIGURE 6.28 *Example of elaboration providing supplemental information.*

In figure 6.29, for example the narrator is describing in his elaboration different obstacles that can prove dangerous to a bicyclist. One such obstacle is the cattle guard. As the signer begins his description, he asks the addressees if they have ever been to a farm. The addressees respond that they have not, which prompts the narrator to continue with the elaboration involving the cattle guard.

Figure 6.29 begins with the narrator finishing his first description of the cattle guard gate. He signs COW CAN'T ESCAPE, which explains the purpose of the gate. He then pauses and asks whether or not the addressees are familiar with what he has described. As he signs KNOW, he shakes his head slightly back and forth to elicit a response from his addressees. In the third line he scans the audience to see their responses. He pauses for .77 seconds and then signs OH-I-SEE to their answer. His eye gaze leaves the addressees and he returns to the story. He returns to the explanation of the fence since the audience does not understand what he had described. KNOW marked the start of the narrator's interaction with the addressees. When his eye gaze turns downward he returns to telling the story. This example demonstrates how narrators sometimes assess whether an addressee understands elements of the narrative.

Narrators also requested information from the addressees. One narrator, for instance, asked an addressee for the name sign for a person in the narrative, shown in figure 6.30. The narrator first produces SIGN, with his eyes directed at his hands. The narrator in the second picture produces a name sign as he looks to the man on his right. He then signs KNOW, "Do you know?" The sequence illustrates how a narrator interacts with an addressee. In this example the signer attempts to remember the name sign of a character. When he is unable to remember, he asks an addressee for help.

MAIN-EVENTS SECTION: NARRATIVE EVENTS AND ELABORATIONS

The main-events section of a narrative is comprised of narrative events that are elaborated upon. We can return to "Junior Year Football," a narrative whose events and elaborations I have already described, and see how the narrative events are elaborated upon using the six different types of elaborations. Table 6.6 lists the four narrative events from the story, along with the elaborations of each event. The type of elaboration is identified as well as the type of narration used. This table reveals how a main event is structured: the narrator moves from describing a narrative

Elaboration:

    COW   CAN'T   ESCAPE
"This prevents the cows from escaping."

Narrator interacting with addressees:

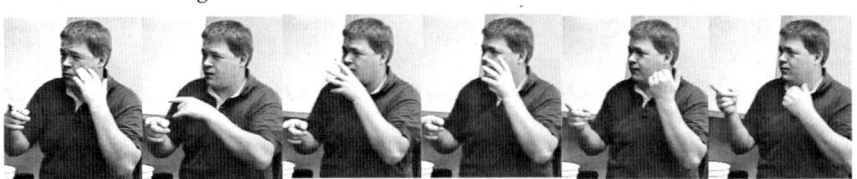

                                                                                     y/n
KNOW   PRO→X   FARM   BEFORE   PRO→X
"Are you familiar with this? Have you been on a farm before?"

Point/Pause   OH-I-SEE
[Watches addressees' responses.]
        "Oh, I see."

Narrator returns to elaboration:

CYLINDRICAL-ENTITY-EXTEND-TO↓L1-L2
"There were poles laid down . . ."

FIGURE 6.29 *Example of narrator interacting with addressees.*

                                                                                               q
SIGN   possible name sign   KNOW
"His name sign? Was it [produces name sign]? Do you know?"

FIGURE 6.30 *Narrator requesting information from addressee.*

TABLE 6.6. *Distribution of T and P Narration in Main-Events Section of "Junior Year Football."*

Narrative event	Elaboration	Elaboration type	T narration	P narration
1. The game started.	We were completely overwhelmed and outplayed.	Expressing emotion	X X	X
2. We lost the game 41 to 11.	It was so embarrassing.	Expressing emotion	X X	X
3. I found out that our opponents had a challenging schedule	"Now you tell us. We should have known this before."	Constructed dialogue	X	
	The captain ruined it for us.	Supplemental information	X	X
	I shouldn't have been all "This is going to be easy."	Expressing emotion	X X	
4. Our coach was furious and bawled out the team.	I close my eyes to shut him out.	Expressing emotion	X	X
	His beating was intense.	Supplemental information	X	
	I can't even repeat what he said to you.	Interaction with addressee	X	X

event to elaborating on the event and then to describing the next narrative event.

The narrator draws on the two types of narration throughout the main-events section. All but one narrative event in "Junior Year Football" is described using T narration. In contrast, elaborations used T and P narration together more often than T narration alone. P narration uses blends that demonstrate or depict events as if they are happening in real space. This feature fits well with elaborations, which flesh out the details of the story. Rather than merely lexically describing what occurred, a narrator may also use P narration to demonstrate the event. An addressee draws on the textual description and the demonstrations to get a more complete understanding of what happened from the perspective of the narrator.

Chapter 7

The Structure of Explication,

Reflection, and Conclusion

Sections in ASL Narratives

Narratives do not end with the main events section. Rather, they continue with up to three more sections, explication, reflection and conclusion. The *explication* section elaborates on one aspect of the main-events section. In the *reflection* section the narrator comments on how he or she feels about what happened in the main events section. The *conclusion* serves to mark the end of the narrative.

EXPLICATION SECTIONS

The narrator does not describe new narrative events in this section. This shift to talking about what happened is accompanied by an increase in T narration over P narration. Table 7.1 lists the types of narration that are used in the explication sections of the 12 narratives. T narration alone is used in 66 percent of the lines produced in explication sections compared to 44 percent of the lines in the main events section. T and P narration together are used in 33 percent of the lines in the explication sections. P narration alone is used in one line, accounting for the final 1 percent.

The explication section conveys fewer different types of information than does the main-events section. Table 7.2 compares the type of information that appears in the four sections described (introduction, background, main events, and explication). I have listed the 22 different types of information conveyed by utterances in the 12 narratives. The utterances produced in the explication section convey 11 different types of information, compared to 21 in the main-events section. The utterances produced in the explication section most often provide supplemental information (28 instances).

TABLE 7.1. Use of T or P Narration or a Combination in the Explication Section.

Section	T narration			T and P narration					P narration			Total
	T	T+Tk	T+S	T+D	T+B	T+Tk+S	T+D+S		D+S	S		
Introduction	18	3	0	0	0	0	0		0	0		21
Background	53	13	10	10	2	0	0		1	6		95
Main event	197	29	167	62	4	3	11		2	34		509
Explication	59	10	20	6	8	0	0		0	1		104

Note: T = T narration, Tk = token blend, S = surrogate blend, B = buoy, D = depicting blend

TABLE 7.2. *Distribution of Information Type Across the Four Narrative Sections.*

Type of information conveyed	Introduction	Background	Main Event	Explication
Physical movement - person	0	9	114	8
Physical movement - vehicle	0	0	8	0
Movement of object	0	1	5	1
Physical movement - animal	0	0	1	0
Supplemental information	3	46	166	28
Identify participant	4	9	9	1
Identify location	3	3	5	0
Identify time	1	3	15	6
Introduce dialogue	0	0	2	0
Period of time	0	1	4	0
Interact w/addressee	1	1	8	0
Constructed dialogue	0	3	48	4
Expression of emotion	0	10	54	13
Mental activity	0	1	12	1
Describe a thing	0	5	12	4
Describe topography	0	0	12	0
Geographic distance	0	0	10	1
Arrangement of people	0	1	7	0
Arrangement of things	0	0	0	0
Mannerism	0	0	4	0
Listing	0	0	1	0
Written text	0	1	3	1
Total different types	5	14	21	11

Ten of the 12 narratives include an explication section, with an average length of 29.8 seconds. The shortest explication section lasts 2 seconds and the lengthiest continues for 75 seconds. This section is an average of 12 lines long, ranging from a single line in one narrative to 32 lines in the longest explication section. On average, the length of this section is almost identical to the length of the background section, in both time and number of lines involved. Extended eye closures mark the end of the explication section; however, in three of the narratives, measurements of eye closures cannot be accurately made because of the direction of the signer's head. The average length of time the eyes remain closed (of the six that could be measured) is .38 seconds, ranging from .26 to .53. The eye closures are accompanied by head nods in four of the explanations. In all three of the narratives produced in a group setting, the eye closures occur during head turns in which the narrator changes whom he or she is looking at.

EXPLICATION SECTION: TALKING ABOUT, NOT DEMONSTRATING

The explication section follows the main-events section, in which the narrator describes and elaborates on the narrative events. Rather than provide new information, the narrator selects a particular narrative event and provides further explanation of it. Table 7.3 lists the focus of each narrative's explication section. For example, the narrator in "Junior Year Football" describes four narrative events, which are listed here:

1. The game started.
2. We lost the game 41 to 11.
3. I found out that our opponents had a challenging schedule
4. Our coach was furious and bawled out the team.

Of the four narrative events, the narrator selects the second one, losing the game, to expand upon in the explication section. This expansion

TABLE 7.3. *Focus of Explication Section of Each Narrative.*

Narrative	Focus of Explication Section
Around the World	Explains how advice received changes his trip
Biathlon	N/A
Biking Over Water	Explains how he could have avoided the problem
Card Game	Explains the losers reaction
Cheerleading	Explains why the squad improved
East Coast Beaches	N/A
Firehouse Fun	Explains how they tell the fire department they spent the night in the firehouse
Flat Tire	Explains how he attempted to help his friend
Junior Year Football	Explains the consequence of losing the game
Left Behind	Explains how he and his friend made-up
Moment of Silence	Explains why the students were crying
Tobacco Story	Explains how principal discovered the student was chewing tobacco

explains the consequence of this loss on the team: it was not selected for post-season play.

The focus of the explication sections is different in each narrative, as the descriptions in table 7.3 demonstrate. However, the sections are similar in that they all provide an explanation of a narrative event described in the preceding main-events section.

T narration predominated in the explication section. Narrators used T narration alone in 69 percent of the lines produced in the explication section. In four of the narratives only T narration was used. The predominant use of T narration fits with the purpose of the explication section, which is to talk about a narrative event rather than demonstrate it. Figure 7.1 is an example of an explication section. The main-event section of this narrative describes how the narrator and his bicycling partner lost a day of travel. They needed to cross a large body of water and the only way to do so was to take a ferry, which ran only once a day—and they had missed the daily trip. In the explication section, the narrator explains how he could have avoided the situation.

The signer's eye gaze is directed toward the addressee throughout the explication section and no blends are created, which is evidence that he is using T narration.[1] This predominant use of T narration is consistent across the explication sections of the 12 narratives. T and P narration together was used in only 25 percent of the lines produced in the explication section. P narration alone occurred in only 6 percent of the lines in the explication sections. T narration is suited for use in the explication section because it is used to talk about events rather than demonstrate events.

Narrators often identify which narrative event the explication section will focus on. The main-event section that preceded the explication section in figure 7.2 describes various lifts and stunts performed by the football cheerleading squad. The audience was impressed with the squad's efforts and congratulated them on the performance. The explication section explains why the cheerleading squad had improved their routines. The first line of this explication section is reproduced in figure 7.2. The narrator identifies that he will explain why the cheerleading squad's performance had improved, which caused the audience to respond enthusiastically. The narrator continues in this explication section to explain what else contributed to the improvement, but this first line illustrates how the topic of this section is introduced.

1. DON'T KNOW is treated as T narration because I cannot clearly see a surrogate blend being used.

PRO-1　　　ADVICE　　　　　PREPARE

READ　　　M-A-P

"My advice would be to read a map and be prepared."

BETTER　　　QUOTE　　　HOMEWORK　　　THEN

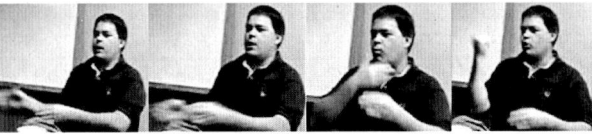

PLAN　　　　　BETTER

"It is better to 'do your homework,' so you can have a good plan."

PRO-1　　　NOT　　　PREPARE

"I wasn't prepared."

PRO-1　　　DON'T KNOW

"I didn't know (how to prepare)."

FIRST　　　DAY　　　　EXPERIENCE　　　　PROGRESS

KNOW

"It was a first-time experience for me, but I made progress, you know."

FIGURE 7.1 *Explication section from "Biking Over Water."*

<u>rhet</u>
WHY   FOR-ALL-THE-TIME-PRIOR GALLAUDET

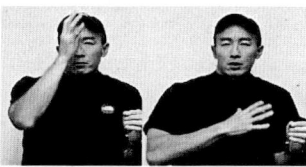

CHEER   NONE   MAN

"Why hadn't these types of stunts been performed?
The Gallaudet cheerleading squad never before had men as members."

FIGURE 7.2 *Identifying the focus of the explication section.*

In the explication section the narrator focuses on what he or she deems the most significant narrative event of the main-events section and explains it in more detail. These explanations were given most often using T narration. The predominant use of T narration reflects that the purpose of this section is to talk about what happened rather than to demonstrate what happened. This characteristic of using T narration contrasts with the use of T and P narration in the reflection section, which provides both textual descriptions and blends.

REFLECTION

Seven of the 12 narratives contain reflection sections, with an average length of 6 seconds. The shortest reflection section lasts 2 seconds and the lengthiest continues for 10 seconds. The average number of lines for this section is 2.5. This varies from 3 lines in the shortest to 6 lines in the longest reflection section. The length of this section is almost identical to the introduction section both in time and in the number of lines involved. Extended eye closures again mark the end of the reflection section. The average length of time the eyes remain closed at the conclusion of the six reflection sections that can be measured was .51 seconds, ranging from .33 to .67 seconds. T narration is used in 55 percent of the lines and 45 percent of the lines are produced with T and P narration. This nearly even division between T narration (10 instances) and P narration (8) shows that narrators both talk about how they felt at the time of the event and demonstrate their remembered reactions. Table 7.4 shows this distribution of T and P narration in the reflection section. Surrogate blends are the only type of blends used in the reflection section. There are 6 instances of T narration and a surrogate blend and two instances of T narration with a token and surrogate blend. This is different from the background, main-events, and explication sections, which all use both surrogate and depicting blends. The reflection section describes how a narrator felt about an experience. Surrogate blends, in which one's face and body postures can blend with the face and body of a person in the past event to demonstrate an emotion, lend themselves to the expression of feelings.

The reflection section conveys four types of information. Table 7.5 lists the type of information provided in the reflection section as compared to the previous four sections. The reflection section conveys supplemental information (7 instances), identifies time (1 instance), offers constructed dialogue (1 instance), and expresses emotion (9 instances). The variety of information conveyed is significantly less than that in the background, main event and explication sections; the narrow focus of conveying one's feelings about past events reduces the type of information that can be conveyed.

REFLECTION SECTION: DESCRIBING AND DEMONSTRATING

The reflection section from "Moment of Silence" (figure 7.3) illustrates the general pattern of narration found in reflection sections. In this narrative the two students in the narrator's class begin to cry during a moment of silence honoring the victims in the Oklahoma City bombing. The narrator finds out later that these students had friends who were killed in the explosion. In the reflection section of this narrative he demonstrates what he was feeling at the moment he saw the students. This is followed by a comment on the experience. The narrator uses T and P narration in the first line of figure 7.3 to describe and demonstrate what he did during the event. His eye gaze is directed toward the |classroom event| with the students, and he signs WOW LOOK-AT$^{\rightarrow\text{|classroom event|}}$ and WONDER. His face blends with his own in the event space and expresses his feeling of being overwhelmed and moved by what he witnessed. In this line he demonstrates and describes for the addressees what he was feeling at the moment of the event. The demonstration consists of his eye gaze directed

TABLE 7.4. Use of T or P Narration or a Combination in the Reflection Section.

Section	T narration				T and P narration				P narration			Total
	T	T+Tk	T+S	T+D	T+B	T+Tk+S	T+D+S	D+S	S			
Introduction	18	3	0	0	0	0	0	0	0			21
Background	53	13	10	10	2	0	0	1	6			95
Main Event	197	29	167	62	4	3	11	2	34			509
Explication	59	10	20	6	8	0	0	0	1			104
Reflection	10	0	6	0	0	2	0	0	0			18

Note: T = T narration, Tk = token blend, S = surrogate blend, B = buoy, D = depicting blend

TABLE 7.5. *Distribution of Information Type Across Five Sections.*

Type of information conveyed	Introduction	Background	Main Event	Explication	Reflection
Physical movement - person	0	9	114	8	0
Physical movement - vehicle	0	0	8	0	0
Movement of object	0	1	5	1	0
Physical movement - animal	0	0	1	0	0
Supplemental information	3	46	166	28	7
Identify participant	4	9	9	1	0
Identify location	3	3	5	0	0
Identify time	1	3	15	6	1
Introduce dialogue	0	0	2	0	0
Period of time	0	1	4	0	0
Interact w/addressee	1	1	8	0	0

Constructed dialogue	0	3	48	4	1
Expression of emotion	0	10	54	13	9
Mental activity	0	1	12	1	0
Describe a thing	0	5	12	4	0
Describe topography	0	0	12	0	0
Geographic distance	0	0	10	1	0
Arrangement of people	0	1	7	0	0
Arrangement of things	0	0	0	0	0
Mannerism	0	0	4	0	0
Listing	0	0	1	0	0
Written text	0	1	3	1	0
Total different types	5	14	21	11	4

WOW   LOOK-AT→|classroom event| WONDER

"As I was looking at this I thought, "Wow, I wonder what that is like."

TOUCH-HEART   WOW

"That experience really touched me."

FIGURE 7.3 *Reflection section from "Moment of Silence."*

at the |classroom event| as if he were looking at the students. The description consists of the signs WOW and WONDER. WOW describes what he was feeling during this past event. WONDER identifies that he was reflecting on what it would be like to lose someone in the explosion as his students had.

He then directs his eye gaze toward the addressee to his right and signs TOUCH-HEART, and then turns his eye gaze toward the addressee on his left and signs WOW. This is an example of T narration, which expresses his reaction to the entire event. He is no longer demonstrating what he did during the past event; rather, he is commenting on the entire past event and how this experience affected him.

The reflection section conveys information about how a narrator felt about certain past events. In so doing, the narrator provides social information to the addressee. He or she states how the events affected him or her or were interpreted at the moment they were experienced. In six of the seven reflection sections the narrator presents a feeling about the past experience twice, once with T narration and once with T and P narration. Although the order of the narration types varied, narrators produce both in the reflection section.

CONCLUDING A NARRATIVE

How a narrator signals the end of a narrative varies slightly depending on whether the narrator was in a group setting or was the only signer.

Signers who were interviewed told several narratives in sequence. The conclusions of these narratives have to distinguish between the end of one narrative and the beginning of the next. Narrators who were part of a group had to identify the end of the narrative to signal to the other participants that another person could take the floor.

Three of the narratives were told in a group setting. The narrators of these stories consistently signal the end of the narrative by lowering their arms and directing their eye gaze toward another participant. In all narratives, at least one (sometimes more than one) participant takes the floor to comment on the narrative. An example of how a narrative ends in a group setting is illustrated in figure 7.4. The narrator (N) ends and turns to the man (M) seated to her right, whom the story was about. The narrator in figure 7.4 ends the narrative and turns to the man on her right to ask if he remembers the incident. As she signs PRO$^{\rightarrow x}$ and taps the man on the arm, another participant's hand is visible indicating that her turn as the primary signer has already ended. The eye gaze of the man seated to the narrator's right is directed toward the signer out of view. The man then begins to comment on the narrative by signing NOT BELIEVE ANY, ADD, ADD. He cautions the other participants not to believe the story they have just seen, as it is an exaggeration of what happened. The narrator responds to this with the sign LIE, to which he waves his hand at as if to say, "Whatever." The fact that three participants are talking, often overlapping each other, is evidence that the original narrator is no longer the primary signer. The narratives told in group settings all concluded in a similar manner. The narrator turns his or her eye gaze to another participant and stops signing. Other participants take up the floor to comment on the preceding narrative.

The narratives that were not told in a group setting end differently. These narrators were telling several narratives one after another. As a result, the conclusions of one narrative had to be distinguished from the beginning of the next. There are two ways this is done. In one, the narrators lowered their arms and stopped signing. In the second, narrators use a sign, such as FINISH, to grammatically encode the end of the narrative.

Nine of the narratives analyzed were produced in such an interview situation. These signers were asked to talk about their past and it was expected that they would have the floor for an extended period of time. In six of these nine, narrators simply lower their arms and pause momentarily. An example of this is illustrated figure 7.5. The last line in the reflection section is TIME FAST. The narrator then lowers his arms and

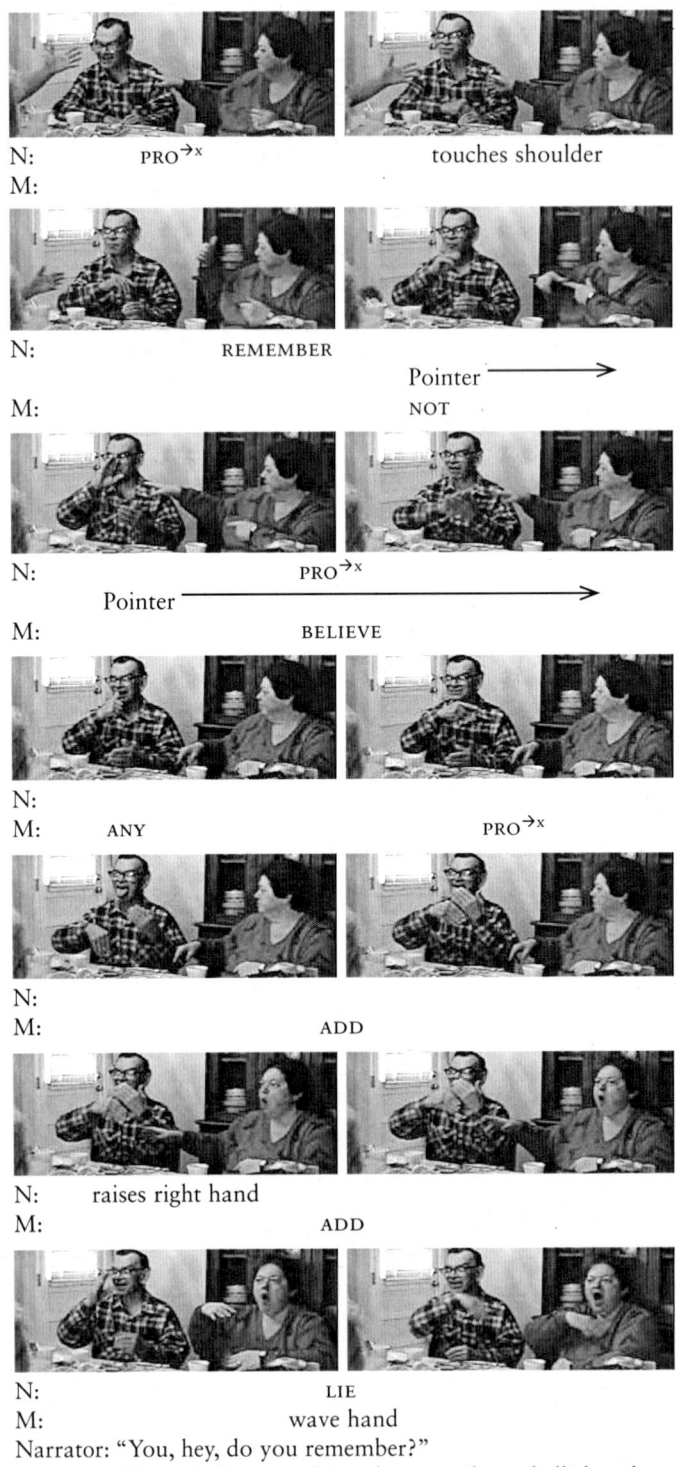

Narrator: "You, hey, do you remember?"
Man: "Don't believe anything she says. She embellishes the story."

FIGURE 7.4 *End of a narrative in a group setting.*

| TIME | FAST | arms lowered |

FIGURE 7.5 *Example of a narrator ending a narrative.*

pauses before continuing on to the next narrative. It appears that an addressee asks him a question about the narrative because he nods his head before continuing.

The narrators in the other three narratives use signs to mark the end of the narrative. The narrator in figure 7.6 has been describing his four years playing college football. He completes the narrative about his junior year on the team, during which one loss results in the team failing to make the NCAA Division III playoffs. The narrative that follows describes his senior year. The last line of the reflection section of his narrative about his junior year is shown in the first line of figure 7.6. The second line shows the transition between the narrative of his junior year and the next one about his senior year. In the last line of the reflection section DEPRESS FINISH, the narrator describes his disappointment that his team did not make the playoffs. He then signs JUNIOR to identify that that was the year he just described. A head nod accompanies the production of this sign. The sign and head nod signal the completion of one story. The sign SENIOR

| DEPRESS | FINISH | drops hands |

"I am so depressed about this being over. Oh well."

                              t
JUNIOR   SENIOR

"That was junior year. Senior year . . ."

FIGURE 7.6 *Narrator using lexical signs to signal the end of one narrative and beginning of the next.*

Explication, Reflection, and Conclusion in ASL Narratives : 143

signals the beginning of the next narrative, which the narrator marks with the nonmanual signal for topics. This example illustrates how a narrator grammatically encodes the end of one narrative and the beginning of another. Narrators also use signs such as FINISH and NEXT to signal the end of a story.

Chapter 8

Conclusion

The goal of this research was to describe how ASL users package experiences and convey them to others in the form of personal narrative. Signers and speakers select among different possible grammatical structures to convey their experiences. These structures can simultaneously express "what happened" along with the narrator's perspective on this experience. Narratives are a means of connecting with others. The involvement of the audience in a narrative is evidence that a connection has been made.

I described two different types of narration. In textual (T) narration, the narrator uses lexical signs to grammatically encode information. The eye gaze is directed toward the addressee and the utterances do not use surrogate or depicting blends. In perceived (P) narration, the narrator does use surrogate and depicting blends. Through blending the signer demonstrates or depicts the actions of a past event in the immediate environment. The eye gaze during P narration may be directed in ways that depict the eye gaze of the surrogate. P narration demonstrates a concrete instance of an event although the signer is not actually repeating the event as they occurred. Bringing past events into the immediate environment allows the addressee to partially witness and interpret the past events. Such active participation creates the involvement necessary for a connection to be made between the narrator and the addressee.

Distinguishing between T and P narration throughout a narrative clarifies the narrator's focus at particular points. Whereas T narration focuses attention on the story, P narration focuses on the narrator's experience of the past events. Narrators use the different types of narration as the information they need to convey changes. An analysis of the common structure of ASL narratives shows that there is a pattern to the use of T and P narration.

THE ORDERED SECTIONS OF ASL NARRATIVES

All 12 of the ASL narratives I analyzed are structured in the same way. Narratives begin with an introduction, which serves two purposes: to secure the floor or mark the beginning of a new story, and to introduce what the narrative will be about. The background section follows the introduction. Its primary function is to orient the addressee, providing basic information such as the topic, the participants in the event, and where the event took place. The narrator then identifies and describes the events in what I have labeled the main-events section. The narrator describes a temporally ordered set of events, providing details about these events with elaborations. The explication section follows and expands or clarifies one of the narrative events. In the reflection section, the narrator comments on how he or she felt about what happened in the main-events section. The narrator then concludes the narrative with a signal that it is finished. Table 8.1 charts the different sections that appeared in each narrative.

All the narratives include introduction, main-event, and conclusion sections; however, background, explication, and reflection are not always present. The absence of a section does not imply an incomplete narrative but suggests that the presence or absence of these sections reflect the range of information that may be included. The specific information within each section varies, but the function of each section and the narrator's use of T and P narration within the sections does not.

The labels that I have given to the sections (introduction, background, main events, explication, reflection, and conclusion) reflect the type of information expressed. They differ from those of Labov and Waletzky (abstract, orientation, complicating action, evaluation, resolution, and coda) in that they more closely reflect the information I found conveyed in the narratives analyzed. For example, complicating action as defined by Labov and Waletzky consists of narrative clauses that recapitulate a sequence of events leading up to their climax, the point of maximum suspense. I did not find that the ASL narrators always build toward a climax; in fact, the location of the climax within the narrative varies. A climax can occur at the beginning of the main event or at the end, and in some narratives the narrator simply conveys a series of events and there is no single climactic point. (I did find consistent the identification of an event and then an expansion of that event.) I did not find examples of codas, or short summaries of the narrative. I propose new labels to highlight that these stories are not rehearsed, carefully structured narratives. Terms such as *abstract*, *complicating action*, and *coda* give the impression that the narrator has a prepared narrative to tell. There are, of course, narratives that are told more than once; these may have a more polished structure that could

TABLE 8.1. *Presence of Sections Across Narratives.*

Narrative	Introduction	Background	Main Event	Explication	Reflection	Conclusion
1. Card Game	X	X	X	X	X	X
2. Moment of Silence	X	X	X	X	X	X
3. Tobacco Story	X		X	X		X
4. Around the World	X	X	X		X	X
5. Biathlon	X	X	X	X	X	X
6. Biking Over Water	X		X	X		X
7. Cheerleading	X	X	X	X	X	X
8. East Coast Beaches	X	X	X		X	X
9. Firehouse Fun	X	X	X	X		X
10. Flat Tires	X	X	X	X		X
11. Junior Year Football	X	X	X	X		X
12. Left Behind	X	X	X	X	X	X

include aspects described as abstracts and codas, but I did not find these in the narratives I analyzed.

The sections in the narratives I analyzed tend to follow the same order (introduction, background, main events, explication, reflection, conclusion), which suggests that there is a preferred ordering of the information. In all 12 narratives, the introductions precede the main events. In one narrative, the background section interrupts the main-events section, because the narrator does not provide the necessary background information prior to the main-event section. He therefore stops relating the main events and provides the necessary background to allow the audience to comprehend the remainder of the main events. This adjusted arrangement of the sections underscores that these narratives were not preplanned. Their structures can be affected by the fact that they are a reflection of the narrator's thought process.

IDENTIFYING SECTIONS

I derived this overall structure from careful analysis of 12 narratives. I first created transcripts of each narrative. In the transcripts I documented what was produced in two ways. I captured the utterance with pictures, which supplemented the English glosses that identified the sign. Using the concept of an "idea unit" (Chafe 1994), I divided the narrative into lines, with each line equivalent to an idea unit. I then described the meaning conveyed in each line. In addition, I identified how this information was expressed: through T narration, surrogate blends, depicting blends, token blends, buoys, or any combination of these.

I found "pauses" between the major sections of the narratives and identified them on the transcripts. Certain behaviors—extended eye closures, head nods, relaxing or lowering of the hands, and a pause in signing—cluster together in narratives and result in a longer pause than that at the end of a single idea unit. Two grammatical structures often follow these behaviors: a lexical sign such as THEN, ANYWAY, or NEXT, and a nonmanual signal for a new topic with the first sign of the subsequent line. I found that pauses occur at the same points in each narrative and extrapolated that the narrative sections contained within the pauses serve the same function across all the narratives. These functions became the labels for the six sections.

DETERMINING MEANING

The core goal of my analysis was to identify the meaning of each utterance, which I needed in order to determine a section's function. I used everything the narrators do to produce each utterance in my interpretation of its meaning—the lexical signs they use, where they direct their signs, and where they direct their eye gaze, as well as their facial expressions, body postures, gestures, and pauses. A signer may not produce any lexical sign to describe his reaction to an event; he may convey his reaction instead simply through his facial expression. The narrator's reactions are significant to comprehending the narrative, so the transcript should reflect them. I found that the most efficient way of incorporating these nontextual features into the transcript was to include still pictures taken from the videotaped narratives.

Utterances often simultaneously convey more than one meaning through the use of both T and P narration. Figure 8.1 provides an example of this. The signer uses T narration with the sign EMBARRASS, which describes his reaction to the event. At the same time that he uses P narration, his face blends with his face during the past event to demonstrate how he was feeling. The facial expression represents a feeling or emotion different from that described by the sign EMBARRASS, something like anguish. An addressee draws on both these structures to comprehend the meaning of the utterance.

Table 8.2 summarizes the type of information that the narratives convey. The categories are, for the most part, self-explanatory. "Movement of a person" includes all utterances that describe how a person moved, regardless of the details of that movement. "Explanation/facts" is not as straightforward. This category became a catchall category for utterances

EMBARRASS
"I was so embarrassed."

FIGURE 8.1 *Simultaneous use of T and P narration.*

Conclusion : 149

TABLE 8.2. *Types of Information Conveyed in the Narratives.*

Type of information	Number of instances across narratives
1. Movement of a person	114
2. Movement of a vehicle	8
3. Movement of an animal	1
4. Movement of an object	5
5. Explanation/facts	159
6. Background information	7
7. Identify participant	9
8. Identify location	5
9. Identify time/time reference	15
10. Identify length of time	4
11. Interact with addressee	8
12. Story management	9
13. Constructed dialogue	48
14. Emotions/feelings	54
15. Mental process	12
16. Description of an object	12
17. Description of topography	12
18. Geographic distance	10
19. Arrangement of people	7
20. Mannerism	4
21. Written text	3

that did not fit into the other 20 categories. Utterances in this category often give additional explanations or details about an event.

The utterance in figure 8.2 helps illustrate this category. The narrator is describing his experience bicycling across the United States. Along the way he meets an experienced cyclist who offers suggestions to improve the signer's performance. The experienced cyclist explains to the signer that he has habits that were hampering him. The utterance PRO-1 CARRY HABIT functions as an explanation for his actions. The utterances in this category are the most varied; however, they all provide this generic type of information and could not be grouped with any of the other categories.

With the transcripts and function tables grouped into sections I looked at the grammatical structures used to convey the information. Recall that every line was coded for the use of textual narration, tokens, depicting

| PRO-1 | CARRY | HABIT |

"I brought my habits (from my college days)."

FIGURE 8.2 *Example of an utterance categorized "Explanations/facts."*

verbs, buoys, and surrogates or combinations of these; for example, the utterance in figure 8.2 uses both T narration and a token blend.

TEXTUAL NARRATION AND PERCEIVED NARRATION

The 12 narratives contain 10 different grammatical structures, or combinations of grammatical and other conceptual structures. Table 8.3 lists these structures, along with the frequency with which they occurred. Some types of information are more commonly expressed with one grammatical or conceptual structure over another, which leads to variation in the use of T or P narration in the different sections.

I combined the grammatical structures with the information types to see how narrators encode different types of information. In table 8.4 the information type is listed in the left column. The table displays the number of times each grammatical structure is used to convey the information type. Grey boxes indicate that no instances of a particular type were used.

TABLE 8.3. *Types and Frequency of Structures Used.*

Grammatical structure	Instances of use
1. Textual description	197
2. Surrogate blend	22
3. Depicting blend	39
4. Textual description + token blend	29
5. Textual description + surrogate blend	167
6. Textual description + depicting blend	35
7. Textual description + buoy	4
8. Textual description + token & surrogate blends	3
9. Textual description + depicting & surrogate blends	11
10. Depicting & surrogate blends	2

TABLE 8.4. *Grammatical Structures Used to Express Information Type.*

Type of information	Narration type									
	TN	S	DV	TN+T	TN+S	TN+DV	TN+B	TN+T+S	TN+DV+S	DV+S
1. Movement of a person	5	10	22		62	6		2	7	1
2. Movement of a vehicle			3		5					
3. Movement of an animal						1				
4. Movement of an object			3			2				
5. Explanation/facts	109			20	14	13	3			
6. Background information	7									
7. Identify participant	4			3	1			1		
8. Identify location	5									
9. Identify time/time ref	13				2					
10. Identify length of time	3				1					
11. Interact with addressee	8									
12. Story management	8					1				
13. Constructed dialogue	9	5		1	33				2	
14. Emotions/feelings	19	6			29					
15. Mental process					12					
16. Description of an object	3		4	2		3				
17. Describe topography			1	2		8			1	
18. Geographic distance	2		1		6					
19. Arrangement of people			5			1			1	1
20. Mannerism	1	1			2					
21. Written text	1			1	2					
Totals	197	22	39	29	168	35	3	3	11	2

The most common way narrators encode all types of information is with textual narration, which occurs in 197 of the lines (39 percent). Utterances that use textual narration and surrogate blends are the next most common, with 168 lines (33 percent). Specific types of information tend to be conveyed with specific structures. For example, to describe the movement of a person, narrators use textual descriptions with surrogate blends in 54 percent of the lines. Similarly, constructed dialogue favors the use of textual narration and surrogate blends; this combination appears in 66 percent of the lines produced. When narrators convey factual information or provide explanations, however, they most frequently use textual narration alone (69 percent).

What my analysis shows is that the grammatical means narrators use to express information is motivated by the type of information conveyed. Events that can be visually demonstrated—running, for example—are encoded using structures that use surrogate blends and depicting verbs. Those events that cannot not be visually demonstrated, such as identifying the name of a participant, are encoded with textual descriptions. I found that these various means of expression are distributed through the six sections of the narrative in another significant pattern. To illustrate how the function of a section influences the narration type used, figure 8.3 shows the distribution of T and P narration in the narrative "Moment of Silence."

Each column in the diagram represents an utterance. Utterances are grouped together into sections. A bar that covers the bottom half of the column represents an utterance that uses T narration alone. A bar that covers the entire column represents the simultaneous use of T and P narration.

The introduction, background, and explication sections of narratives focus on providing "factual" information about the main events. In these sections, narrators use T narration alone more often than P narration. In the main-events and reflection sections, narrators describe events or reactions to events using T and P narration. In the main-events sections, narrators elaborate on the narrative events, frequently providing details by demonstrating an aspect of the event. For instance, for the narrative event that describes a student spitting tobacco out of a classroom window, the elaboration demonstrates the student's behavior or the wad of tobacco moving through the window. These elaborations consistently used surrogate and depicting blends, which brought the past events to the immediate environment. The concreteness of these blends is what allows an addressee

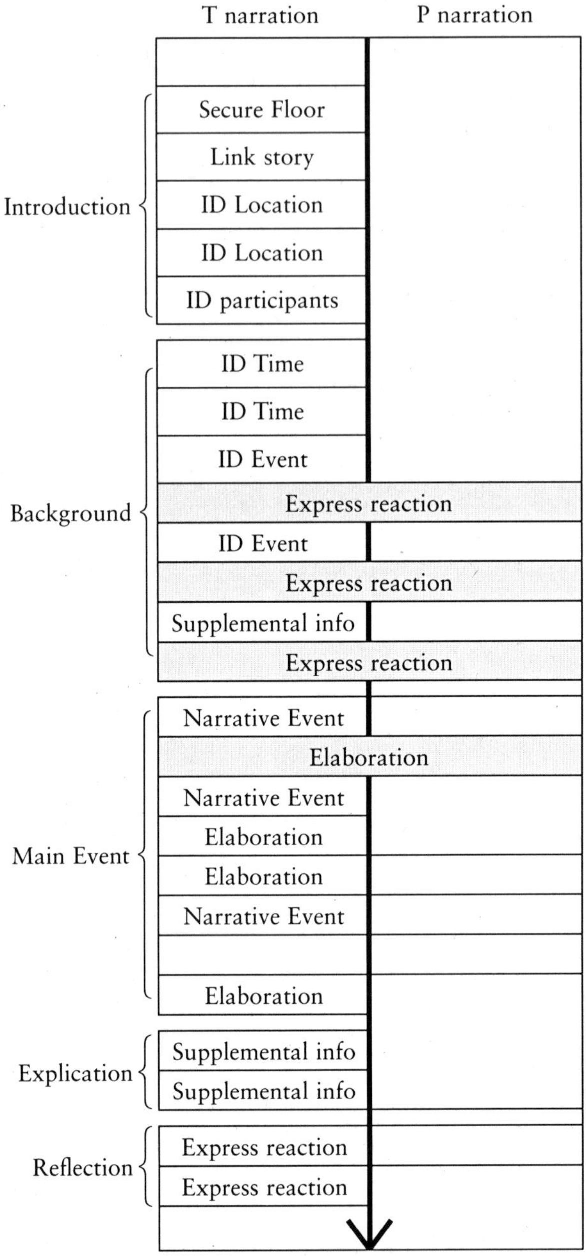

	T narration	P narration
Introduction	Secure Floor	
	Link story	
	ID Location	
	ID Location	
	ID participants	
Background	ID Time	
	ID Time	
	ID Event	
		Express reaction
	ID Event	
		Express reaction
	Supplemental info	
		Express reaction
Main Event	Narrative Event	
		Elaboration
	Narrative Event	
	Elaboration	
	Elaboration	
	Narrative Event	
	Elaboration	
Explication	Supplemental info	
	Supplemental info	
Reflection	Express reaction	
	Express reaction	

FIGURE 8.3 *Distribution of T and P narration in the narrative "Moment of Silence."*

to become "involved" in the narrative because they, in essence, see a bit of the past event.

WHAT CONSTITUTES DATA FOR ANALYSIS?

The objective of my research was to describe the structure of personal narratives in ASL. I could not have performed my analysis without including several features traditionally not defined as linguistic.

Direction of Eye Gaze

The direction of eye gaze assists in distinguishing the use of T and P narration. When signers conceptualize surrogate or depicting spaces, the direction of their eye gaze provides clues to recognize these structures. An eye gaze directed away from an addressee, for instance toward an imagined entity in the signing space, signals to the addressee that the narrator is providing a partial visual demonstration of the past events.

With P narration, eye gaze direction provides further information about whose constructed dialogue the signer was representing. I used figure 8.4, an exchange between principal and student, to illustrate constructed dialogue between two characters in chapter 6. In describing this exchange,

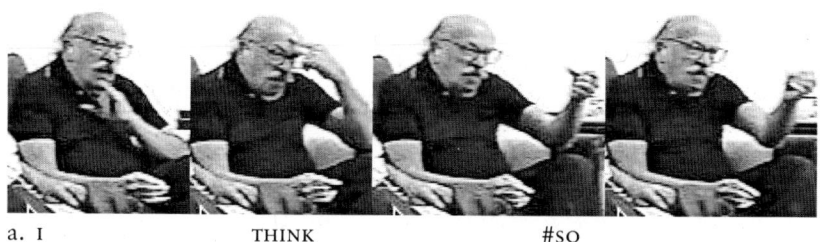

a. I   THINK   #SO
Principal: "I thought so!"

b. HOW   KNOW   PRO→|principal|
Student: "How did you know?"

FIGURE 8.4 *Eye gaze used to identify signer.*

the narrator does not grammatically encode the identity of the surrogate signer; he simply provides the constructed dialogue from the past event. The direction of his eye gaze assists the addressee in identifying the identity of the surrogate signer. In figure 8.4a the surrogate |principal|'s eye gaze is directed downward toward a surrogate |student|. The surrogate |student|'s eye gaze in figure 8.4b is directed upward toward the surrogate |principal|. This change in eye gaze direction indicates that the narrator is representing the dialogue of two different surrogates.

These surrogate blends are used to make aspects of the past event partially visible to an addressee.

Facial Expressions

Facial expressions are also critical in this analysis. As with eye gaze, facial expressions provide information necessary to identify when a signer is creating a blend. The blending of the signer's face with a character in a past event contributes to the addressee's understanding that the signer is providing a partial visual representation of what happened during the past event. In figure 8.4 the change in facial expression helps signal that the signer is producing in the event space what another character said.

As the signer in figure 8.5 produces the topic CAPTAIN DET$^{\rightarrow x}$ his face is neutral. His facial expression changes when he produces PRO$^{\rightarrow |opponent|}$ NOTHING. This change, accompanied by the shift in body position and the way in which he articulates the signs, signals the creation of a blend.

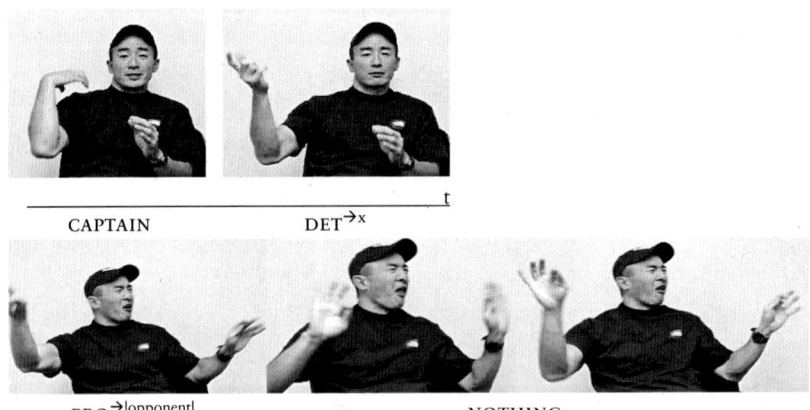

"The captain said, 'That team is nothing.'"

FIGURE 8.5 *Facial expression change signaling different narration type.*

Open and close mouth

FIGURE 8.6 *Demonstration of behavior without using lexical signs.*

Demonstrations

There are instances during which a signer does not produce any signs, but rather demonstrates the actions of a character from the past event. Figure 8.6 provides an example of this. The narrator in Figure 8.6 is demonstrating the students' responses to the principal's request that they prove they were not chewing tobacco. The signer does not grammatically encode what each student did; instead, he provides a demonstration of their behavior. The addressee uses the demonstration to understand what happened. These instances of P narration are as important to the understanding of the narrative as T narration and therefore need to be included in the analysis.

Not only are these non-lexical features necessary to understanding the meaning of the narrative, which is essential to performing an analysis, they also enhance the telling of the narrative. People tell narratives to share their thoughts and feelings about a past event. *Why* a story is told is often more important than *what* the story is about. The social components are as significant as the factual components. In the narratives I analyzed signers convey social and factual aspects of the narratives using P narration, which is signaled by features that have traditionally been excluded from the analysis of ASL narratives—in effect, researchers have been excluding important components of ASL narratives. To effectively understand language in use, the definition of language must be expanded to include all the features necessary for analysis.

NARRATIVE EVENTS VS. SOCIAL INFORMATION

The primary focus of my research was on the overall structure of ASL personal narratives. This is a necessary initial step in understanding how ASL narrators convey information, both factual and social, in their narratives. Although I do not provide a detailed analysis of instances in which social information is conveyed, I do point out several instances in which it was and where this type of information is likely to be found. The narratives analyzed in this volume demonstrate that T narration is most often used to convey narrative events (that is, the factual aspects of the narrative), and P narration is most often used when the narrator prefers to in some way demonstrate the event for the addressee. These demonstrations allow the addressee to partially perceive the events and therefore interpret for him- or herself what happened.

Other aspects of how narrators produce their stories, however, give insight into the social information a narrator is conveying. For example, narrators consistently demonstrate with their facial expressions how a person reacted to a situation. The narrator in "The Tobacco Story" does not use T narration to simply state that he and his classmates were shocked and surprised that their principal discovered that a student was spitting tobacco out the classroom window; instead, he relies on P narration to convey this.

In "Around the World" the narrator describes his experience meeting another bicyclist during a cross-country bicycle journey. The narrator learns that this other cyclist is almost finished biking around the world. His journey has taken over nine years and the cyclist has amassed a lot of knowledge in this time. He offers the narrator several suggestions that have a positive impact on the narrator personally and on his enjoyment of his own trip. As the narrative progresses, so does the narrator's admiration for the other cyclist. He begins to direct signs such as THANK-YOU and ADVICE in space in a way that reflects this social component of admiration. When the narrator articulates the sign THANK-YOU he directs it upward toward the area associated with the cyclist. This upward direction is not part of the normal production of the sign; however, it suggests that the narrator is conceptualizing the experienced cyclist as someone who is more knowledgeable and whom he respects. By directing the sign upward the narrator incorporates this social aspect into the narrative without overtly stating it. Continued analysis of ASL narratives will find additional ways narrators package social information within narrative events. The contributions of both T and P narration must be included in these analyses as both contribute factual and social components to the narratives.

CONCLUSION

This research has made several contributions to our understanding of narratives in general and ASL personal narratives in particular. I have described the overall structure of ASL personal narratives, which I identified from the narratives themselves rather than look for characteristics of narrative structures found in spoken languages. The process of moving from the narratives to the structure highlighted the fact that although the structures of the ASL narratives are similar to those for spoken languages, some aspects are unique.

Another contribution of this research is the illustration of the importance of analyzing everything a signer produces. It is not enough to rely on the lexical signs produced. One must also use eye gaze, gestures, facial expression, and the direction of signs to comprehend the meaning of a narrative. It is necessary to correctly understand the meaning of the narrative before any analysis can take place. Further, the ways in which signs are articulated, for example, where they are directed, can convey social information by embedding it into the narrative.

The importance of including all aspects of what is produced by the narrator is also a contribution to narrative analysis in general. Traditionally, the analysis of spoken narratives has relied on what was said, on the words. The ways in which the words were uttered, the intonation, volume, or pitch, have not been incorporated consistently into the analysis. Further, the narrator's facial expressions, eye gaze, and gestures have also been omitted. The inclusion of these behaviors will likely expand our understanding of spoken narratives and give further insight into their structure.

This research has laid a foundation for expanding our understanding of personal narratives. We can, for instance, begin to examine how narratives vary depending on who the audience is: What events are foregrounded when a story is relayed to a close friend compared with a story told to new acquaintance?

Further, we can now look at what linguistic structures are used to tell stories. I have shown that narrators rely on P narration most when they are conveying the main events of their experience. Each narrator examined deftly moved between T and P narration to effectively convey their stories, making use of complex linguistic forms in the telling of everyday events. Through this examination of ASL narratives we see how the extraordinary develops from the ordinary: when signers relay the ordinary events of their daily life by sharing personal narratives with others, they do so in extraordinary ways.

References

Ahlgren, Inger, and Brita Bergman. 1990. Preliminaries on narrative discourse in Swedish sign language. In *Current trends in European sign language research: Proceedings of the 3rd European Congress on Sign Language Research*, ed. T. Vollhaber, 261–67. Hamburg: Signum Verlag.

———. 1994. Reference in narratives. In *Perspectives on sign language structures: Papers from the 5th International Symposium on Sign Language Research*, Vol. 1, ed. Inger Ahlgren, Brita Bergman, and Mary Brennan, 29–36. Durham, England: ISLA.

Bahan, Ben and Sam Suppalla. 1994. American Sign Language Literature Series Collector's Edition, Teacher's Videotape and Student Videotape *Bird of a Different Feather and For a Decent Living*. San Diego, CA: Dawn Pictures.

Bahan, Ben, and Sam Supalla. 1995. Line segmentation and narrative structure. In *Language, gesture, and space*, ed. Karen Emmorey and J. Reilly, 171–91. Hillsdale, NJ: Lawrence Erlbaum.

Bailey, Charles James. 1981. Theory, description and differences among linguists (or, what keeps linguistics from becoming a science). *Language and Communication* 1:39–66.

———. 1987. Variation theory and so-called "socio-linguistics" grammar. *Language and Communication* 7 (4):269–91.

Baker, Charlotte. 1977. Regulators and turn-taking in American Sign Language. In *On the other hand: New perspectives on American Sign Language*, ed. Lynn Friedman, 215–36. New York: Academic Press.

Bamberg, Michael. 1991. Narrative activity as perspective-taking: The role of emotionals, negation and voice in the construction of the story realm. *Journal of Cognitive Psychotherapy* 5 (4): 275–90.

Barthes, Roland. 1966. Introduction à l'analyse structurale des récits. *Communications* 8:1–27.

Bell, Allan. 1984. Language style as audience design. *Language in Society* 13 (2):145–204.

Briggs, Charles, and Richard Bauman. 1992. Genre, intertextuality and social power. *Journal of Linguistic Anthropology* 2 (2): 131–72.

Brown, Gillian, and George Yule. 1983. *Discourse analysis*. Cambridge, UK: Cambridge University Press.

Bucholtz, Mary. 2000. The politics of transcription. *Journal of Pragmatics* 32:1439–65.

Capps, Lisa, and Elinor Ochs. 1995. Out of place: Narrative insights into agoraphobia. *Discourse Processes* 19:407–39.

Chafe, Wallace. 1974. Language and consciousness. *Language* 50:111–13.

———. 1980. The deployment of consciousness in the production of a narrative. In *The pear stories*, 9–50. Norwood, NJ: Ablex.

———. 1985. Information flow in Seneca and English. In *Proceedings of the 11th annual meeting of the Berkeley Linguistics Society*, ed. Mary Niepokuj, Mary Van Clay, Vassiliki Nikiforidou, and Deborah Feder, 14–24. Berkeley, CA: Berkeley Linguistics Society.

———. 1994. *Discourse, consciousness, and time: The flow and displacement of conscious experience in speaking and writing.* Chicago: University of Chicago Press.

Chomsky, Noam. 1957. *Syntactic structures.* The Hague: Mouton.

———. 1965. *Aspects of the theory of syntax.* Cambridge, MA: MIT Press.

———. 1981. *Lectures on government and binding.* Dordrecht, The Netherlands: Foris.

Dematteo, Asa. 1977. Visual imagery and visual analogues. In *On the other hand: New perspectives on ASL*, ed. Lynn Friedman, 109–36. New York: Academic Press.

Dressler, Richard, and Roger Kreuz. 2000. Transcribing oral discourse: A survey and model system. *Discourse Processes* 29 (1): 25–36.

Dry, Helen. 1981. Sentence aspect and the movement of narrative time. *Text* 1:230–40.

Dudis, Paul. 2004. Body partitioning and real-space blends. *Cognitive Linguistics* 15 (2): 223–38.

Edwards, Jane, and Martin Lampert, ed. 1992. *Talking data: Transcription and coding in discourse research.* Hillsdale, NJ: Lawrence Erlbaum Associates.

Ekman, Paul. 1999. Basic emotions. In *Handbook of Cognition and Emotion*, ed. Tim Dalgleish and Mick Powers, 45–60. Sussex: John Wiley and Sons.

Ekman, Paul, and W. F. Friesen. 1975. *Unmasking the face: A guide to recognizing emotion from facial clues.* New Jersey: Prentice Hall.

Engberg-Pedersen, Elisabeth. 1993. *Space in Danish sign language: The semantics and morphosyntax of the use of space in a visual language.* Hamburg, Germany: Signum.

———. 1999. Path- and ground-denoting expressions in descriptions of motion events in Danish sign language. Paper presented at the 6th International Cognitive Linguistics Conference, Stockholm, Sweden.

Fasold, Ralph. 1984. *Sociolinguistics in society.* Oxford, UK: Blackwell.

———. 1990. *Sociolinguistics in language.* Oxford, UK: Blackwell.

Fauconnier, Gilles. 1985. *Mental spaces.* Cambridge, MA: MIT Press. Repr., Cambridge, UK: Cambridge University Press, 1994.

———. 1997. *Mappings in thought and language.* Cambridge, UK: Cambridge University Press.

Fauconnier, Gilles, and Mark Turner. 1994. Conceptual projection and middle spaces. UCSD Cognitive Science Technical Report, University of California, San Diego.

Fauconnier, Gilles and Mark Turner. 1996. Blending as a central process of grammar. In *Conceptual Structure, Discourse and Language* ed. Adele Goldberg, 113–30. Stanford, CA: CSLIL Publications.

Fillmore, Charles. 1982. Frame semantics. In *Linguistics in the morning calm*, ed. Linguistic Society of Korea, 113–37. Seoul: Hanshin.

———. 1985. Frames and the semantics of understanding. *Quaderni di semantica* 6 (2): 222–53.

Fridman, Boris, and Scott Liddell. 1998. Sequencing mental spaces in an ASL narrative. In *Discourse and cognition: Bridging the gap*, ed. Jean-Pierre Koenig, 255–68. Stanford, CA: CSLI Publications.

Gee, James. 1986. Units in the production of discourse. *Discourse Processes* 9 (4): 391–422.

———. 1991. A linguistic approach to narrative. *Journal of Narrative and Life History* 1 (1): 15–39.

Gee, James, and Judy Kegl. 1983. Narrative/story structure, pausing, and American Sign Language. *Discourse Processes* 6(3): 243–58.

Gibbs, Raymond. 2003. Embodied experience and linguistics meaning. *Brain and Language* 84:1–15.

Gilet, Peter. 1998. Vladimir Propp and the universal folktale: Recommissioning an old paradigm—Story as initiation. *Middlebury Studies in Russian Language and Literature* 17. New York: Peter Lang.

Gumperz, John. 1982. *Language and social identity*. Cambridge, UK: Cambridge University Press.

Gumperz, John, and Dell Hymes. 1972. *Directions in sociolinguistics: The ethnography of communication*. New York and London: Holt, Rinehart and Winston.

Hinrichs, Erhard, and Livia Polanyi. 1986. Pointing the way: A unified treatment of referential gestures in interactive discourse. *Papers from the Parasession on Pragmatics and Grammatical Theory at the 22nd Regional Meetings of the Chicago Linguistic Society*, 298–314. Chicago: Chicago Linguistic Society.

Hymes, Dell. 1974. Why linguistics needs sociolinguistics. In *Foundations in sociolinguistics: An ethnographic approach*, 69–82. Philadelphia: University of Pennsylvania Press.

———. 1981. *In vain I tried to tell you: Essays in Native American ethnopoetics*. Philadelphia: University of Pennsylvania Press.

Jefferson, Gail. 1979. A technique for inviting laughter and its subsequent acceptance/declination. In *Everyday language: Studies in ethnomethodology*, ed. G. Psathas, 79–96. New York: Irvington Publishers.

———. 1983. Issues in the transcription of naturally occurring talk: Caricature versus capturing pronunciation particulars. *Tilburg Papers in Language and Literature* 34:1–12.

Johnstone, Barbara. 1987. "He says...so I said": Verb tense alternation and narrative depictions of authority in American English. *Linguistics* 25:33–52.

Joos, Martin. 1964. *The English verb*. Madison: University of Wisconsin Press.

Kendon, Adam. 2004. *Gestures*. Cambridge, UK: Cambridge University Press.

Key, Mary Ritchie. 1975. *Paralinguistics and kinesics (Nonverbal communication)*. Metuchen, NJ: Scarecrow Press.

Kintsch, Walter, and Teun A. van Dijk. 1975. How one remembers and summarizes stories. *Language* 9 (40): 98–116.

Klima, Edward S., and Ursula Bellugi. 1979. *The signs of language*. Cambridge, MA: Harvard University Press.

Labov, William. 1972. *Language and the inner city*. Philadelphia: University of Pennsylvania Press.

———. 1981. Speech actions and reactions in personal narrative. In *Analyzing Discourse: Text and talk: Georgetown University Round Table*, ed. Deborah Schiffrin, 219–47. Washington, DC: Georgetown University Press.

———. 1997. Some further steps in narrative analysis. *Journal of Narrative and Life History* 7:395–415.

Labov, William, and J. Waletzky. 1967. Narrative analysis: Oral versions of personal narratives. *Essays on the verbal and visual arts: Proceedings of the 1966 annual meeting of the American Ethnological Society*, ed. June Helm, 12–44. Seattle: University of Washington Press.

Lakoff, George. 1987. *Woman, fire, and dangerous things: What categories reveal about the mind*. Chicago: University of Chicago Press.

Lakoff, George, and Mark Johnson. 1980. *Metaphors we live by*. Chicago: University of Chicago Press.

Langacker, Ronald W. 1987. *Foundations of cognitive grammar*. Vol. 1, *Theoretical prerequisites*. Stanford, CA: Stanford University Press.

———. 1991. *Foundations of cognitive grammar*. Vol. 2, *Descriptive application*. Stanford, CA: Stanford University Press.

Lavandera, Beatriz. 1978. Where does the sociolinguistics variable stop? *Language in Society* 7 (2): 171–82.

Leech, Geoffery. 1971. *Meaning and the English verb*. London: Longman.

Lévi-Strauss, Claude. 1955. The structural study of myth. *Journal of American Folklore* 68:428–44.

———. 1964. *Mythologiques: Le cru et le cuit*. Paris: Plon.

———. 1966. *Mythologiques: Du miel aux cendres*. Paris: Plon.

Liddell, Scott. K. 1995. Real, surrogate, and token space: Grammatical consequences in ASL. In *Language, gesture and space*, ed. Karen Emmorery and Judy Reilly, 19–41. Hillsdale, NJ: Lawrence Erlbaum.

———. 2003. *Grammar, gesture and meaning in American Sign Language*. Cambridge, UK: Cambridge University Press.

Liddell, Scott, and Melanie Metzger. 1998. Gesture in sign language discourse. *Journal of Pragmatics* 30:657–97.

Macaulay, Ronald. 1991. "Coz it isny spelt when they say it": Displaying dialect in writing. *American Speech* 66 (3):280–91.

Mather, Susan, and Elizabeth Winston. Spatial mapping and involvement in ASL storytelling. In *Pinky extension, eye gaze, and other intricacies: Language use in deaf communities*, ed. Ceil Lucas, 170–82. Washington, DC: Gallaudet University Press.

McNeill, David. 1992. *Hand and mind: What gestures reveal about thought*. Chicago: University of Chicago Press.

———. 1999. An Ontogenetic universal and several cross-linguistic differences in thinking for speaking. Paper presented at the 6th International Cognitive Linguistics Conference, Stockholm, Sweden.

Metzger, Melanie. 1995. Constructed dialogue, constructed action in ASL. *Sociolinguistics in deaf communities*, ed. Ceil Lucas, 255–71. Washington, DC: Gallaudet University Press.

Metzger, Melanie, and Ben Bahan. 2001. Discourse analysis. In *The sociolinguistics of sign language*, ed. Ceil Lucas, 112–45. Cambridge, UK: Cambridge University Press:

Miller, Christopher. 2000. Iconic and metaphorical mappings in multichannel syntax and discourse: Simultaneity and handedness alternations in LSQ. Lecture given at the 28th LAUD Symposium, Landau, Germany.

Miller, Christopher, and Marion Blondel. 1998. Spatial superstructure, rhythm and metaphor in a performance narrative: The Tortoise and the Hare. Lecture given at the 6th International Conference of Theoretical Issues in Sign Language Research, Washington, DC.

Ochs, Elinor. 1979. Transcription as theory. In *Developmental Pragmatics*, ed. Elinor Ochs and Bambi B. Schieffelin, 43–72. New York: Academic Press.

Padden, Carol. 1986. Verbs and role-shifting in ASL. In *Proceedings of the 4th National Symposium on Sign Language Research and Teaching*, ed. Carol Padden, 44–57. Washington, DC: National Association of the Deaf.

Palmer, Frank R. 1965. *A linguistic study of the English verb*. London: Longman.

Polanyi, Livia. 1981. What stories can tell us about their tellers' world. *Poetics Today* 2:97–112.

———. 1982. Literary complexity in everyday storytelling. In *Spoken and written language: Exploring orality and literacy*, ed. Deborah Tannen, 155–170. Westport, CT: Ablex Publishing.

———. 1985. A theory of discourse structure and discourse coherence. In *Proceedings of the 21st annual meeting of the Chicago Linguistics Society*, 306–22. Chicago: University of Chicago, Department of Linguistics.

Poulin, Christine, and Christopher Miller. 1995. On narrative discourse and point of view in Quebec Sign Language. In *Language, gesture and space*, ed. Karen Emmorey and Judy S. Reilly, 117–31. Hillsdale, NJ: Erlbaum.

Propp, Vladimir. 1968. *Morphology of the folktale*. Austin: University of Texas Press.

Rayman, Jennifer. 1999. Storytelling in the visual mode: A comparison of ASL and English. In *Storytelling and conversation: Discourse in deaf communities*, ed. Elizabeth Wilson, 59–82. Washington, DC: Gallaudet University Press.

Roberts, Celia. 1997. Transcribing talk: Issues of representation. *TESOL Quarterly* 31:167–72.

Rosch, Eleanor. 1977. Human categorization. In *Advances in cross-cultural psychology*, ed. Neil Warren, 1–72. London: Academic Press.

Sacks, Harvey, Emanuel Schegloff, and Gail Jefferson. 1974. A simplest systematics for the organization of turn-taking for conversation. *Language* 50:696–735.

Sapir, Edward. 1929. The status of linguistics as a science. *Language* 5:203–14.

Schiffrin, Deborah. 1981. Tense variation in narrative. *Language* 57 (1): 45–62.

———. 1984. How a story says what it means and does. *Text* 4 (4): 313–46.

———. 1987. *Discourse markers*. Cambridge, UK: Cambridge University Press.

———. 1994. *Approaches to discourse analysis*. Cambridge, UK: Cambridge University Press.

———. 2002. Mother and friends in a Holocaust life story. *Language in Society* 31:309–53.

Schiffrin, Deborah, Deborah. Tannen, and Heidi. Hamilton. 2001. *The handbook of discourse analysis*. Malden, MA: Blackwell.

Stokoe, William C. 1960. Sign language structure: An outline of the visual communication system of the American deaf. Studies in Linguistics Occasional Papers 8, Department of Anthropology and Linguistics, University of Buffalo.

Stokoe, William C., Dorothy Casterline, and Carl Cronberg. 1965. *The dictionary of American Sign Language on linguistic principles*. Washington, DC: Gallaudet College Press. Rev. ed., Silver Spring, MD: Linstok Press, 1978.

Supalla, Ted. 1978. Morphology of verbs of motion and location in American Sign Language. In *American Sign Language in a bilingual, bicultural context: Proceedings of the 2nd annual national symposium on sign language research and teaching*, ed. Frank Caccamise and Dion Hicks, 27–45. Silver Spring, MD: National Association of the Deaf.

———. 1986. The classifier system in American Sign Language. In *Noun classes and categorization*, ed. Colette Craig, 181–213. Philadelphia: John Benjamin.

———. 1990. Serial verbs of motion in ASL. In *Theoretical Issues in Sign Language Research*. Vol. 1, *Linguistics,* ed. Susan Fischer and Patricia Siple, 127–52. Chicago: University of Chicago Press.

Talmy, Leonard. 1985. Lexicalization patterns: semantic structure in lexical forms. In *Language typology and syntactic description*. Vol. 3, *Grammatical Categories and the Lexicon*, ed. Timothy Shopen, 36–149. Cambride, UK: Cambridge University Press.

———. 1991. Paths to realization: A typology of event conflation. In *Proceedings of the 17th annual meeting of the Berkeley Linguistics Society*, 480–519. Berkeley: Berkeley Linguistics Society.

Tannen, Deborah. 1986. Introducing constructed dialogue in Greek and American conversational and literary narrative. In *Reported speech across languages*, ed. Florian Coulmas, 311–32. The Hague: Mouton.

———. 1989. *Talking voices: Repetition, dialogue, and imagery in conversational discourse*. Cambridge, UK: Cambridge University Press.

Taub, Sarah. 2001 *Language from the body: Iconicity and metaphor in American Sign Language*. Cambridge, UK: Cambridge University Press.

Taub, Sarah, and Dennis Galvan. 2001. Patterns of conceptual encoding in ASL motion descriptions. *Sign Language Studies* 1 (2): 175–200.

Turner, Mark, and Gilles Fauconnier. 1995. Conceptual integration and formal expression. *Journal of Metaphor and Symbolic Activity* 10 (3): 183–204.

Trudgill, Peter. 1984. *Applied sociolinguistics*. New York: Academic Press.

van Dijk, Teun A. 1976. Narrative macro-structures: Logical and cognitive foundations. *Journal for Description Poetics and Theory of Literature* 1:547–568.

———. 1977. *Text and context: Explorations in the semantics and pragmatics of discourse*. London: Longman.

———. 1980. *Macrostructures: An interdisciplinary study of global structures in discourse, interaction and cognition*. Hillsdale, NJ: Lawrence Erlbaum.

Van Hoek, Karen. 1992. Conceptual spaces and pronominal reference in American Sign Language. *Nordic Journal of Linguistics* 15:183–99.

———. 1996. Conceptual locations for reference in American Sign Language. In *Spaces, Worlds and Grammar*, ed. Gilles Fauconnier and Eve Sweetser, 334–50. Chicago: Chicago University Press.

Wardhaugh, Ronald. 1998. *An introduction to sociolinguistics*. 4th ed. Oxford, UK: Blackwell.

Wilson, Julie M. 1996. The tobacco story: Narrative structure in an ASL story. In *Multicultural aspects of sociolinguistics in deaf communities*, ed. Ceil Lucas, 152–80. Washington, DC: Gallaudet University Press.

Winston, Elizabeth. 1991. Spatial referencing and cohesion in ASL text. *Sign Language Studies* 73:397–410.

Wulf, Alyssa, and Paul Dudis. 2005. Body partitioning in ASL metaphorical blends. *Sign Language Studies* 5 (3): 317–32.

Wulf, Alyssa, Paul Dudis, Robert Bayley, and Ceil Lucas. 1999. Null subject variation in ASL narratives. Paper presented at New Ways of Analyzing Variation (NWAV) Conference: Toronto.

Appendix

Transcription Conventions: Identifying Signs from Liddell 2003

CAT	A single uppercase English word identifies a single ASL sign. Using the gloss CAT does not mean that the sign has the same morphological, syntactic, or semantic characteristics as the English word *cat*.
OH-I-SEE	Uppercase English words separated by hyphens also represent a single sign.
BOY^SAME	The symbol ^ indicates that two signs have been combined into a single compound sign.
B-U-D-G-E-T	Hyphens between uppercase letters indicate a sequence of alphabetic character signs used to spell a word.
#WHAT	A word beginning with the symbol # indicates a lexical sign whose origin is ultimately traceable to a sequence of alphabetic character signs.
PRO-1	The notation -1 indicates a first person form. In this case, the sign is the first person singular pronoun.
{TWO}{O'CLOCK}	A sign composed of the two bound morphemes {TWO} and {O'CLOCK}
{AGE_0}-FOUR	A sign composed of the prefix {AGE_0} – combined with the root FOUR.
WAIT[DURATIONAL]	A sign derived from WAIT. The label in the square brackets identifies the grammatical process underlying the sign being represented.
_____t $SIGN_1$......$SIGN_n$	The sequence of signs from $SIGN_1$ to $SIGN_n$ is accompanied by the nonmanual signal t.
'this week'	A gesture, that in the context of its use, has the significance 'this week'.
$SIGN_1$ ... $SIGN_n$ THEME----------	The top line represents the signing of the strong hand while the bottom line represents the signing of the weak hand. Here, the weak hand maintains the THEME buoy in place during the sign sequence $SIGN_1$ ... $SIGN_n$.

Notational Convention: Direction and Placement from Liddell 2003

PRO$^{\to x}$	$^{\to x}$ indicates that the sign is directed toward entity x. Entity x will be either an element of real space or a real-space blend.
|PRINCIPAL|	Enclosing a word in vertical brackets identifies an entity in a real-space blend.
PRO-$^{\to|student|}$	$^{\to|student|}$ indicates that the sign is directed toward the blended entity |student|.
PRO-PL$^{\supset a,b,c}$	$^{\supset a,b,c}$ indicates that the hand moves along a path, such that the extent of the path points toward entities a, b, and c
SAY-NO-TO-1$^{\cup x}$	$^{\cup x}$ indicates that the head and eyes are directed toward entity x.
HONOR$^{\cup \to y}$	$^{\cup \to y}$ indicats that face and eyes ($^{\cup}$) as well as the hands ($^{\to}$) are directed toward y.
GIVE$^{x \to y}$	$^{x \to y}$ indicates that the sign begins nearer to and/or directed toward x, then moves toward y.
MOVE$^{L1 \to L2}$	$^{L1 \to L2}$ indicates that the hand begins directed toward L1 and ends directed toward L2.
TIME-BREAK$^{\to D2 \downarrow D3}$	$^{\to D2 \downarrow D3}$ identifies a location between D2 and D3. Thus, this sign is directed toward a location between D2 and D3.
INVITE$^{\leftarrow y}$	$^{\leftarrow y}$ indicates that the verb begins directed toward y then moves away from y.
BORROW$^{x \leftarrow y}$	$^{x \leftarrow y}$ indicates that the sign begins nearer to and/or directed toward y, then moves toward x.
INFORM$^{[RECIP]x \leftrightarrow y}$	$^{x \leftrightarrow y}$ indicates that the hands move in opposite directions between x and y. In this sign, each hand produces only a single movement. In producing a one-handed sign such as SAME-DUAL $x \leftrightarrow y$, the hand moves back and forth between x and y.
GO$^{\to}$	$^{\to}$ The sign points in the direction of the action.
THROW$^{\to L}$	$^{\to L}$ The sign is directed toward location L.
[COLLEGE]$^{\to L}$	[]$^{\to L}$ The nondirectional sign enclosed in the square brackets is directed toward location L.
[FIVE]$^{\to addressee}$	[]$^{\to addressee}$ The nondirectional sign enclosed in the square brackets is directed toward the addressee.
[PEOPLE-LINE]$^{\to L1-L2}$	[]$^{\to L1-L2}$ The nondirectional sign enclosed in the square brackets is produced between L1 and L2.
VEHICLE-BE-AT$^{\downarrow L1}$	$^{\downarrow L1}$ The sign is produced at L1.
VEHICLE-DRIVE-TO$^{\downarrow L1-L2}$	$^{\downarrow L1-L2}$ The movment of the sign begins at L1 and ends at L2.
ANIMAL-BE-AT$^{\downarrow on|fence|}$	$^{\downarrow on|fence|}$ The strong hand places the sign at a location on the blended entity |fence|.
FENCE-SURFACE$^{\downarrow L2}$	$^{\downarrow L2}$ The depicting buoy is produced at L2.

Index

Page numbers with a "t" and "f" denote tables and figures respectively.

affect, expressing, 118–20, 127t, 136, 140
"Around the World," 71t, 81t, 87–94, 132t, 147t, 158
audiences
    familiarity, 5–6
    interaction with, 4, 124–25, 126f, 127t
    knowledge base, 78–79, 80, 82
    size effect, 140–43
authority figures, 8–10, 30

background section
    about, 56–60, 78–80, 146
    background knowledge, 84–91
    information type, 97t, 131t
    participants, 81t, 82–84
    P narration, 84–85, 91–94, 96t, 153, 154f
    setting, 79–82
    T narration, 84, 91–95, 96t, 153, 154f
Bahan, Ben, 11, 13
"Biathlon," 71t, 81t, 147t
"Biking Over Water," 71t, 81t, 132t, 133, 134f, 147t
blends, 23–25
    See also specific blends, such as surrogate blends
body position
    in demonstration of action, 106–13
    impact on meaning, 45–46
    in P narration, 62–66
    in surrogate blends, 25f, 26f, 28–29, 107
    See also partitioning, body
buoys, 31–33, 151t, 152t

"Card Game," 80f, 81t, 82, 123, 124f, 132t, 147t

Chafe, Wallace, 5, 50–51
character role, 17, 34–36
"Cheerleading," 71t, 81t, 82, 132t, 133, 135f, 147t
climax, 146
concluding narratives, 69, 140–44, 146
constructed action, 14–15, 16t
constructed dialogue
    about, 6, 114–17, 118t
    narrator modes and, 34–36
    P narration, 116–17, 127t, 153
    T narration, 127t, 153
    types in ASL, 14–15, 16t
    verb tense in, 7–9

depicting blends
    about, 30–34
    in descriptions, 110–13, 123f
    frequency of use, 151t
    information type and, 152t, 153, 154f
    narrator modes and, 36, 37f
    in P narration, 37–38, 145
    transcription of, 49–50
descriptions, 17, 106–14, 120–22, 123f, 157
direct quotes, 114–15

"East Coast Beaches," 71t, 81t, 91, 92, 147t
elaborations
    about, 98–103
    audience interaction, 124–25, 126f, 127t
    constructed dialogue, 114–17, 118t, 127t
    descriptions, 120–22, 123f
    emotional expression, 118–20, 127t, 136, 140
    P narration, 127t, 128, 153, 154f

elaborations (*continued*)
  supplemental information, 123, 124f, 127t, 129, 131t
  T narration, 127t, 128, 153, 154f
  See also movement
emotional expression, 118–20, 127t, 136, 140
evaluative clauses, 3, 34
event space, 22, 26–27, 37
explication section
  about, 67, 68f, 129–35
  information type, 131t
  P narration, 129, 130t, 133, 153, 154f
  surrogate blends, 136, 137t
  T narration, 129, 130t, 133, 134f, 135, 153, 154f
eye closure, 52, 72, 79, 97–98, 131–32, 135
eye gaze
  impact on meaning, 45–47
  line identification and, 11, 13
  narrator modes and, 35
  in P narration, 37, 38f, 57–58, 59f, 145, 155–56
  in surrogate blends, 25f, 26f, 27–29, 108–9, 155–56
  in T narration, 37, 38f, 54–56, 57–58, 59f
  in turn-taking, 54

facial expressions
  emotions, 118–19
  impact on meaning, 45–46
  in movement description, 111–12
  in P narration, 62–66, 156
  in surrogate blends, 25f, 26f, 27–29
Fauconnier, Gilles, 22–23
fingerspelling, 48–49
"Firehouse Fun," 71t, 81t, 85–87, 92, 132t, 147t
"Flat Tire," 71t, 81t, 132t, 147t
foreshadowing, 71t, 78
fragment buoys, 31–33
free clauses, 3

Gee, James, 11, 12f, 13
gestures, 17–21, 22–23, 47–48
  See also blends
glosses, 41–45

hand perseveration, 83
historical present, 6–10, 34
Hymes, Dell, 5

image documentation, 42–48
indirect speech, 117, 118f
information type, 97, 131t, 138–39t, 147t, 149–54
introducers, 114–15
introductory section
  about, 53–56, 70–78, 145–46
  information type, 97t, 131t
  P narration, 96t, 153, 154f
  T narration, 96t, 153, 154f

Johnstone, Barbara, 8–9
"Junior Year Football," 71t, 81t, 98–100, 101f, 125, 127t, 128, 132, 147t

Kegl, Judy, 11, 12f, 13
Kendon, Adam, 19–20
Kintsch, Walter, 4

Labov, William, 2–5, 6–7, 146
"Left Behind," 71t, 81t, 132t, 147t
Lévi-Strauss, Claude, 2
Liddell, Scott, 17–18, 20, 23, 31, 35, 43
line identification, 10–11, 13, 50–51
locomotion, 110–14

main-events section
  about, 60–66, 67f, 95, 96t, 146
  audience interaction, 124–25, 126f
  constructed dialogue, 114–17, 118t
  descriptions, 120–22
  emotional expression, 118–20
  information type, 97t, 131t
  movement, 106–14
  participants, 103–4

P narration, 95, 96t, 98–102, 127t, 128, 153, 154f
  setting, 103–5
  supplemental information, 123, 124f
  T narration, 95, 96t, 98–102, 127t, 128, 153, 154f
McNeill, David, 19–20
mental space theory, 22–23
Metzger, Melanie, 14–15, 16t, 20
"Moment of Silence," 53–70, 71t, 81t, 132t, 136, 140, 147t, 153, 154t
movement
  description of action, 17, 106–14, 157
  locomotion, 110–14
  narrator modes and, 36, 37f
  non-locomotion, 105–10, 113t
  See also depicting blends

narration types, 37–39
  See also P narration; T narration
narrative analysis
  about, 51–52
  data sources, 40–41
  glosses, 41–45
  images in, 42–48
  line identification, 10–11, 13, 50–51
  paralinguistic information in, 18–21, 155–57, 159
  transcription conventions, 48–50, 169–70
narrative clauses, 3
narrative structure
  background section, 56–60, 78–91, 95, 96t, 131t, 146, 153, 154f
  conclusion, 69, 140–44, 146
  explication section, 67, 68f, 129–35, 131t, 153, 154f
  historical present and, 6–10, 34
  introduction, 53–56, 70–78, 95, 96t, 97t, 131t, 145–46, 153, 154f
  main-events section, 60–66, 67f, 95–128, 131t, 146, 153, 154f
  ordered sections, 145–48
  reflection section, 67–69, 135–40, 146, 153, 154f
  research overview, 1–5
narrator modes, 15, 17, 34–36, 37f
narrator role, 15, 17, 34–36, 37f
non-locomotion, 105–10, 113t

paralinguistic information, 18–21, 155–57, 159
participants, 71t, 76–77, 81t, 82–84, 103–4
partitioning, body
  in depicting blends, 33–34
  narrator modes and, 35
  in surrogate blends, 25f, 26f, 29
  in T/P simultaneous narration, 38–39
pauses, 11, 13, 52, 148
perceived narration. *See* P narration
picture documentation, 42–48
P narration
  about, 37–39, 145
  background section, 84–85, 91–94, 96t, 153, 154f
  body position, 62–66
  constructed dialogue, 116–17, 127t, 153
  elaborations, 127t, 128, 153, 154f
  emotional expression, 118–20
  explication section, 129, 130t, 133, 153, 154f
  eye gaze, 37, 38f, 57–58, 59f, 145, 155–56
  facial expressions, 62–66, 156
  frequency of use, 151, 153
  information type and, 152t, 153, 154f
  introductory section, 96t, 153, 154f
  main-events section, 95, 96t, 98–102, 127t, 128, 153, 154f
  in movement description, 113t, 114
  reflection section, 135–37, 140
  social information in, 158
  surrogate blends, 37–39, 145
Propp, Vladimir, 1

Rayman, Jennifer, 15, 17
real space, 22–24
  See also blends
real space blends. See blends
referential clauses, 3
reflection section, 67–69, 135–40, 146, 153, 154f

Schiffrin, Deborah, 7, 9, 34
setting, 71t, 77, 78f, 79–82, 103–5
shapes, 31, 32f, 33
social information, 117, 157–58
spatial conceptualizations, 17–18, 20, 22–23, 31–32
  See also blends
Supalla, Sam, 11, 13
supplemental information, 123, 124f, 127t, 129, 131t
surrogate blends
  about, 25–29, 30, 34
  body position, 25f, 26f, 28–29, 107
  constructed dialogue, 116–17
  explication section, 136, 137t
  eye gaze, 25f, 26f, 27–29, 108–9, 155–56
  facial expressions, 25f, 26f, 27–29
  frequency of use, 151, 153
  information type and, 152t, 153, 154f
  in movement description, 106–10, 113
  narrator modes and, 34–36
  in P narration, 37–39, 145

Tannen, Deborah, 6, 14
textual narration. See T narration
time, expression of, 105
T narration
  about, 37–39, 145
  background section, 84, 91–95, 96t, 153, 154f
  in descriptions, 113t, 114, 122, 123f
  elaborations, 127t, 128, 153, 154f
  emotional expression, 118–20
  explication section, 129, 130t, 133, 134f, 135, 153, 154f
  eye gaze, 37, 38f, 54–56, 57–58, 59f
  frequency of use, 151, 153
  indirect speech, 117, 118f
  information type and, 152t, 153, 154f
  introductory section, 96t, 153, 154f
  main-events section, 95, 96t, 98–102, 127t, 128, 153, 154f
  reflection section, 135–37, 140
  supplemental information, 123, 124f
"Tobacco Story," 13, 35, 38, 47, 71t, 80, 81t, 100, 102, 108–9, 112, 116, 132t, 147t, 158
token space blends
  about, 29–30
  frequency of use, 151t
  information type and, 152t
  in introductions, 55–56
  participant identification, 83, 104
topic identification, 71t, 75–76, 80, 81t, 133, 135f
topic markings, 71t, 73–74, 75f
transcription
  conventions, 48–50, 169–70
  glosses in, 41–45
  images in, 42–48
turn-taking, 53–54, 71t, 72–73, 141, 142f

van Dijk, Teun A., 4
verb tenses, 6–10
  See also depicting blends

Waletzky, J., 2–5, 6–7, 146
Wilson, Judy, 13–14